Play and Playwork

Bringing together authors from a range of academic disciplines and research backgrounds – united as standard-bearers for the child's right to play – and set against a backdrop evoking play's critical essence, this book documents the rise and fall of an explosive period of political interest in play in the United Kingdom.

Has the withdrawal of so much state funding damaged the playwork profession forever? Has the battle for recognition of the significance of play in child development been lost? Why is children's happiness always so low on the agendas of our politicians? The invaluable contributions in this book identify the lessons learned, and the opportunities that may be available to those determined to maintain the struggle for a greater recognition of the importance of children's play in an era defined by the oppressive politics of austerity.

The chapters in this book were originally published as a special issue of the *International Journal of Play*.

Fraser Brown is the first Professor of Playwork and teaches on the Playwork degree course at Leeds Beckett University, UK. He is the specialist link tutor for APAC's postgraduate play therapy courses, and has presented at conferences across the United Kingdom and around the world. His publications include *Play and Playwork: 101 Stories of Children Playing* (2014).

Mike Wragg is a Senior Lecturer at Leeds Beckett University, UK, and the Chair of two charitable trusts: Eccleshill Adventure Playground and New Hall Prison Visitors' Play Facility, both of which have been subject of his recent publications in the *International Journal of Play* and in the *Prison Service Journal*.

Play and Playwork

Notes and Reflections in a Time of Austerity

Edited by
Fraser Brown and Mike Wragg

LONDON AND NEW YORK

First published 2018
by Routledge
2 Park Square, Milton Park, Abingdon, Oxon, OX14 4RN, UK

and by Routledge
711 Third Avenue, New York, NY 10017, USA

Routledge is an imprint of the Taylor & Francis Group, an informa business

© 2018 Taylor & Francis

British Library Cataloguing in Publication Data
A catalogue record for this book is available from the British Library

ISBN 13: 978-1-138-48938-7

Typeset in Times New Roman PS
by diacriTech, Chennai

Publisher's Note
The publisher accepts responsibility for any inconsistencies that may have arisen during the conversion of this book from journal articles to book chapters, namely the possible inclusion of journal terminology.

Disclaimer
Every effort has been made to contact copyright holders for their permission to reprint material in this book. The publishers would be grateful to hear from any copyright holder who is not here acknowledged and will undertake to rectify any errors or omissions in future editions of this book.

Contents

Citation Information   vii
Notes on Contributors   xi

Editorial   1
Fraser Brown and Mike Wragg

1   The state of playwork   3
    Adrian Voce

2   Memories of and reflections on play   10
    Tracy R. Gleason

    Seminar Papers: Best of times to worst of times? Appraising the changing
    landscape of play in the UK

3   Complex geographies of play provision dis/investment across the UK   14
    *John H. McKendrick, Peter Kraftl, Sarah Mills, Stefanie Gregorius and
    Grace Sykes*

4   Play in the good times: the (English) inside story   22
    Tim Gill

5   The Big Lottery Fund's *Children's Play Programme*: a missed opportunity to
    gather the evidence?   27
    Alexandra Long

6   Slip sliding away: a case study of the impact of public sector cuts on some of the
    services supporting children's play opportunities in the city of Sheffield in the
    north of England   32
    Helen Woolley

7   Playwork practitioners' perceptions of the impact on play of austerity in the UK:
    comparing experiences in Scotland and SW England   38
    John H. McKendrick and Chris Martin

CONTENTS

8   Supporting healthy street play on a budget: a winner from every perspective   52
    Alice Ferguson and Angie Page

9   Opportunities for free play   56
    Rob Wheway

10 Promoting playfulness in publicly initiated scientific research: for and beyond
    times of crisis   61
    Cindy Regalado

11 'Strategic playwork': a possibility that is neither 'intervention playwork'
    nor 'environmental playwork'   71
    Arthur Battram

12 Geographies for play in austere times   77
    *John H. McKendrick, Peter Kraftl, Sarah Mills, Stefanie Gregorius and
    Grace Sykes*

    Articles

13 Sharing playwork identities: research across the UK's field of playwork   85
    Sylwyn Guilbaud

14 Ethical practice for the playwork practitioner   100
    David Stonehouse

15 The Big Swing: reflections on the first 10 years of an adventure playground   110
    Mike Wragg

16 Books worth (re)reading:
    Adventure Playgrounds, by Jack Lambert and Jenny Pearson   119
    Fraser Brown

    Index   121

Citation Information

The chapters in this book were originally published in the *International Journal of Play*, volume 4, issue 3 (December 2015). When citing this material, please use the original page numbering for each article, as follows:

Introduction
Editorial
Fraser Brown and Mike Wragg
International Journal of Play, volume 4, issue 3 (December 2015) pp. 215–216

Chapter 1
The state of playwork
Adrian Voce
International Journal of Play, volume 4, issue 3 (December 2015) pp. 217–223

Chapter 2
Memories of and reflections on play
Tracy R. Gleason
International Journal of Play, volume 4, issue 3 (December 2015) pp. 224–227

Chapter 3
Complex geographies of play provision dis/investment across the UK
John H. McKendrick, Peter Kraftl, Sarah Mills, Stefanie Gregorius and Grace Sykes
International Journal of Play, volume 4, issue 3 (December 2015) pp. 228–235

Chapter 4
Play in the good times: the (English) inside story
Tim Gill
International Journal of Play, volume 4, issue 3 (December 2015) pp. 236–240

Chapter 5
The Big Lottery Fund's Children's Play Programme: a missed opportunity to gather the evidence?
Alexandra Long
International Journal of Play, volume 4, issue 3 (December 2015) pp. 241–245

Chapter 6
Slip sliding away: a case study of the impact of public sector cuts on some of the services supporting children's play opportunities in the city of Sheffield in the north of England
Helen Woolley
International Journal of Play, volume 4, issue 3 (December 2015) pp. 246–251

Chapter 7
Playwork practitioners' perceptions of the impact on play of austerity in the UK: comparing experiences in Scotland and SW England
John H. McKendrick and Chris Martin
International Journal of Play, volume 4, issue 3 (December 2015) pp. 252–265

Chapter 8
Supporting healthy street play on a budget: a winner from every perspective
Alice Ferguson and Angie Page
International Journal of Play, volume 4, issue 3 (December 2015) pp. 266–269

Chapter 9
Opportunities for free play
Rob Wheway
International Journal of Play, volume 4, issue 3 (December 2015) pp. 270–274

Chapter 10
Promoting playfulness in publicly initiated scientific research: for and beyond times of crisis
Cindy Regalado
International Journal of Play, volume 4, issue 3 (December 2015) pp. 275–284

Chapter 11
'Strategic playwork': a possibility that is neither 'intervention playwork' nor 'environmental playwork'
Arthur Battram
International Journal of Play, volume 4, issue 3 (December 2015) pp. 285–290

Chapter 12
Geographies for play in austere times
John H. McKendrick, Peter Kraftl, Sarah Mills, Stefanie Gregorius and Grace Sykes
International Journal of Play, volume 4, issue 3 (December 2015) pp. 291–298

Chapter 13
Sharing playwork identities: research across the UK's field of playwork
Sylwyn Guilbaud
International Journal of Play, volume 4, issue 3 (December 2015) pp. 299–313

Chapter 14
Ethical practice for the playwork practitioner
David Stonehouse
International Journal of Play, volume 4, issue 3 (December 2015) pp. 314–323

CITATION INFORMATION

Chapter 15

The Big Swing: reflections on the first 10 years of an adventure playground
Mike Wragg
International Journal of Play, volume 4, issue 3 (December 2015) pp. 324–332

Chapter 16

Books worth (re)reading:
Adventure Playgrounds, by Jack Lambert and Jenny Pearson
Fraser Brown
International Journal of Play, volume 4, issue 3 (December 2015) pp. 333–334

For any permission-related enquiries please visit:
http://www.tandfonline.com/page/help/permissions

Notes on Contributors

Arthur Battram is a management educator, coach, writer, teacher and 'trainer'. He is the author of *Navigating Complexity: The Essential Guide to Complexity Theory in Business and Management* (2007). He speaks regularly on issues including complexity, management and local government.

Fraser Brown is the first Professor of Playwork and teaches on the Childhood Development and Playwork degree course at Leeds Beckett University, UK. He is the specialist link tutor for APAC's postgraduate play therapy courses, and has presented at conferences across the United Kingdom and around the world. His publications include *Play and Playwork: 101 Stories of Children Playing* (2014).

Alice Ferguson is Managing Director of Playing Out, a project she started with Amy Rose, a neighbour from the city of Bristol. This has developed into a community interest company with a national presence across the United Kingdom.

Tim Gill is an independent researcher, writer and consultant whose work focuses on children's play and free time. He is the author of *No Fear: Growing Up in a Risk Averse Society* (2007). He was director of the Children's Play Council (now Play England) from 1997 to 2004.

Tracy R. Gleason is Professor of Psychology at Wellesley College, MA, USA. She is a developmental psychologist, and her research focuses on the relationships that some preschool-aged children have with imaginary companions.

Stefanie Gregorius is a postdoctoral research associate in the School of Tropical Medicine, University of Liverpool, UK. Her work focuses on reducing health care barriers for people affected by disabilities and chronic lung diseases in Malawi and Sudan.

Sylwyn Guilbaud has worked in various playwork roles, and in 2011 completed her PhD, titled 'A phenomenological inquiry into the possibility of played-with-ness in experiences with things'. Alongside her freelance play and playwork research, she is an artist creating small stitched magical beings in support of children's playing relationship with the elements.

Peter Kraftl is Professor and Chair in Human Geography at the University of Birmingham, UK. His research focuses on children's geographies, in particular the emotions, affects, materialities and practices that make up their everyday lives.

Alexandra Long is Course Director of Childhood Development and Playwork at Leeds Beckett University, UK. She is currently undertaking a PhD exploring the impact of the commissioning process on the delivery of children's play services.

Chris Martin is a postgraduate researcher in the Department of Geography at the University of Leicester, UK. His research interests are in cultural geography, centred on children's play and playwork. He is currently undertaking a PhD, researching children and young people's interactions with mobile digital technology in their outdoor play.

John H. McKendrick is Professor in the School for Business and Society at Glasgow Caledonian University, UK. His primary research interests are on poverty (with a particular interest in children) and children's play.

Sarah Mills is Senior Lecturer in Human Geography at Loughborough University, UK. Her research focuses on the geographies of youth citizenship, informal education and volunteering in both contemporary and historical contexts.

Angie Page is Professor of Physical Activity and Public Health at the University of Bristol, UK. Her research interests include physical activity, sedentary behaviour and health outcomes, with an additional focus on the determinants of children's physical activity and eating behaviour.

Cindy Regalado is a doctoral candidate in the Extreme Citizen Science research group at University College London, UK. She also works with CitizenswithoutBorders. This work seeks to create spaces as opportunities (communicatively, physically, emotionally, intellectually, digitally) that incite reflection, exploration and challenging ourselves and our relationships with the world around us.

David Stonehouse is Lecturer in Children and Young People's Nursing, School of Health and Society, University of Salford. A qualified nurse, he is currently undertaking a PhD at Leeds Beckett University, UK, studying 'The Analytical Exploration of Pre-registration Children's Nurses in Children's Play in Both the Academic and Clinical Setting'.

Grace Sykes is research associate in media, communications and sociology at the University of Leicester. Her research interests include educational learning environments, youth engagement and provision, active learning, and transitions to university and employability.

Adrian Voce is a former playworker, inclusive play trainer and now a writer, consultant and campaigner for children's right to play. He is the author of *Policy for Play* (2015) and President of the European Network for Child Friendly Cities and on the boards of the Playwork Foundation and Playing Out. He was awarded an OBE for services to children in 2011.

Rob Wheway is Director of the Children's Play Advisory Service. He has carried out non-interactive observational research of children at play at over 70 areas of housing in England and Wales, each one followed up with consultations with parents and children.

Helen Woolley is Reader in Landscape Architecture and Society at the University of Sheffield, UK. Her research focuses on both strategic issues of green and open spaces and people's relationship with those open spaces in their daily lives. She is the author of *Urban Open Spaces* (2003).

Mike Wragg is a Senior Lecturer at Leeds Beckett University, and the Chair of two charitable trusts: Eccleshill Adventure Playground and New Hall Prison Visitors' Play Facility, both of which have been subject of his recent publications in the *International Journal of Play* and in the *Prison Service Journal*.

EDITORIAL

The term 'austerity', depending on one's view, refers either to government policy designed to stimulate economic growth by reducing public expenditure, or to an ideologically driven process of unnecessary budget cuts designed to reduce the influence of the State and disperse wealth towards those at the top of the income distribution scale.

Irrespective of one's position on the subject of austerity, it is undeniable that those most reliant on public services are going to be most adversely affected when those same services are withdrawn. One of the most reliant and therefore disadvantaged groups, largely by dint of their disenfranchisement and diminished status within UK society, is the nation's children and young people.

Austerity policies are predicted to increase child poverty by a third to its highest level in a generation by 2020, and the Supreme Court has ruled that those same policies are a breach of the United Nations Convention on the Rights of the Child. Local authorities have seen central government budgets for children and youth services reduced, in some cases, by as much as 80%, and provision for children's play is often the first to be withdrawn. Furthermore, government's deregulation of childcare in a bid to reduce cost to parents is, not unsurprisingly, predicted to lead to a reduction in quality of care and experience of the child recipients.

These outcomes arguably represent a sad indictment on the way in which children and young people are valued in UK society, but perhaps more alarmingly it illustrates the gross ignorance of those in command when it comes to understanding children's play. We now know that far from being the trivial behaviour it has been popularly dismissed as, play is in fact a crucial developmental function and evolutionarily developed bio-psychological drive.

Our understanding of the harmful consequences of the suppression of other human drives and impulses, such as to sleep or socialise, for instance, has led to their forced constraint being legislated against in international law. Yet we continue to place restrictions on children's freedoms to play despite the mounting cost to individuals, families and wider society. Increased prevalence of type-2 diabetes, obesity and mental ill-health are all attributed variously to the effects of insufficient play in children's lives.

For some years, employers have been noting an absence in university graduates of the 'soft' employability skills of communication, creativity and teamwork, which are again all attributed to insufficient play in the childhoods of those graduates. Companies at the forefront of global economic growth industries are encouraging play and playfulness in the workplace to both enable employees to overcome their skills deficiencies and as a means of generating creativity and innovation.

The consequences of austerity, such as the mounting number of children growing up in poverty, are often justified as a necessary and short-term pain to be endured in the pursuit of the long-term gain of future economic prosperity. But, as examined within this Special Edition, legislating against play brings about immediate and lasting pain wholly disproportionate to the costs saved. However, perhaps the ultimate price of austerity will be paid by a generation of play deprived, unhealthy, unhappy and under-skilled future adults.

Fraser Brown

Mike Wragg

The state of playwork

Adrian Voce

Playwork in the UK is an approach to working with children in free play settings – and a body of theory and practice informing that approach – that emerged and has traditionally flourished in public play provision, funded to a greater or lesser extent by the state. After the ambitious 12-year play strategy (2008) of the last Labour government seemed to promise a bright future for such services, and for the professional development of the playwork community, the austerity measures of the coalition and Conservative governments since 2010 have greatly reduced the extent of staffed play provision in the public and voluntary sectors; and pushed this emergent profession into seeming decline. Conversely, there is evidence of playwork's growing influence and popularity in other parts of the world; but for the playwork community to withstand the dramatic downturn in its fortunes in the UK, it needs to unify, consolidate its resources, learn from its history and grow and retain control of its own support and representational structures. A new independent vehicle, emerging from a 2013 summit in Sheffield – called to find a response to the existential crisis facing playwork – may be the start of this fight-back.

When I was asked a few years ago to contribute to the book, *Foundations of playwork* (Brown & Taylor, 2008), one result was a chapter called 'The state of play' (Voce, 2008). This was, of course, a pun. Even had I been qualified to write it, one chapter would have been woefully insufficient to do justice to such a vast and complex subject. Thankfully (for writer and reader) my small contribution was limited to the question of how the UK government[1] was responding – or not – to children's play needs at that time. The title of this current consideration of playwork and its challenges may not be quite so obviously invested with wordplay (no pun intended!); but the role of the government must nevertheless feature prominently.

This is because playwork is an approach to working with children in inclusive, open-access spaces – ideally free of charge[2] – within services that must inevitably therefore depend to a large extent on state funding. The inexorable squeeze on such resources since 2010 is the unavoidable context for our analysis, as it is for so much public and voluntary sector activity in the age of austerity.

Originally, as it emerged on the adventure playgrounds of the 1960s, 1970s and 1980s, playwork was a local, grass roots response to the growing need of urban children to have their space to play protected and supported within increasingly dense, spatially deprived inner city neighbourhoods. Voluntary action would lead to fundraising to employ staff and acquire tools and other resources, but sustainable finance needed longer-term funding streams and although many of the adventure playgrounds in which playwork developed were – and still are – independently managed by local charities, they have long depended upon local authority grants and (more latterly) contracts for the lion's share of their usually meagre funds. Still more of them came under direct council management.

Rarely a high priority for local authority funding in their own right (Cole-Hamilton & Gill, 2000) and with no proper statutory basis, playwork services during the 1990s tended to become increasingly overshadowed – and in many cases annexed – by the National Childcare Strategy, as the government made a priority of subsidising not just nursery schools for the children of working parents, but before- and after-school care for their primary-aged children too. Thus, playwork eventually became part of the growth in state provision for children and families that had its apogee in the New Labour Government's Every Child Matters policy (HM Treasury, 2003) – although it was not until the subsequent Children's Plan (Department for Children, Schools And Families [DCSF], 2007), and its promise of a national play strategy, that ministers fully embraced the principle that 'enjoy and achieve' did not simply mean doing well at school.

In the *Foundations of playwork*, Brown and Taylor (2008), noting the arrival shortly before that volume's publication, of the national Play Strategy (Department for Children, Schools and Families/Department for Culture, Media and Sport [DCSF/DCMS], 2008), which 'for the first time in a government document … saw importance given to the role of playworkers', hailed a 'moment of optimism' for the play movement. As a pioneer in higher education for this emerging profession, he was encouraged, no doubt, by the strategy's commitment to create 4000 new playworkers, including 'a core of professionally qualified new graduate leaders' (DCSF/DCMS, 2008).

There were reasons to be cheerful, too, about the 'Play Pathfinder' programme which was to create 30 new staffed adventure playgrounds within top-tier local authorities, whose key strategic staff would also be trained and challenged to develop the crosscutting local play strategies that would aim to transform the public realm for children by embedding playwork perspectives within the planning and commissioning processes for both children's services and playable, child-friendly public space (DCSF, 2010).

The Play Strategy was a 12-year plan, underpinned by an initial investment of £235m for the first three years, to ensure that every neighbourhood in England offered 'a variety of supervised and unsupervised places for play, free of charge' and that the wider public space was welcoming, safe and attractive for children and their play. The influence of the fixed-equipment playground sector notwithstanding,[3] playwork and its allies were in the vanguard of the movement that led to the adoption of this ambitious vision by the national government, and had the strategy been sustained for its full duration, could look forward to the prospect, as Brown had anticipated, of becoming an increasingly important part of the children's workforce.

How things have changed. The Children's Rights Alliance for England (CRAE, 2015) has reported that 'children's play has been a casualty of the austerity drive (as) councils have disproportionately targeted play services for cuts, with many long-standing services and projects closed and the land redeveloped'. CRAE attributes this decline – which it very conservatively[4] quantifies as an overall reduction of 54% in funding for play by local authorities between 2010 and 2014 – directly to the Conservative-led coalition government abandoning the Play Strategy after barely two years, and dropping play from ministerial portfolios altogether for the first time since the early 1980s.

Apart from the large scale reduction in services that these figures represent, the Cameron government, as CRAE also notes, has 'withdrawn recognition of playwork in out-of-school care', leaving many children effectively in school – or under equivalent 'arrangements' – for up to 10-hours a day.

Where this leaves playwork is without the policy, funding or regulatory frameworks that create the demand for it; and the unexpected Conservative victory of May 2015 augurs no respite whatever the Children's Play Policy Forum (CPPF, 2015) may hope for in the way of 'support for staffed play provision to test social prescription models for ... health and well-being initiatives'. Only seven years after Brown's 'moment of optimism', playwork, in England at least, would appear to be in something of an existential crisis. How should we respond?

This was the question earnestly put by the independent researcher and theorist, Bob Hughes and Professor Perry Else, when they invited others in the field to a summit at the University of Sheffield Hallam in the summer of 2013. Hughes and Else called their meeting 'The Argument for Playwork' and suggested that our main problem was that we had not yet conveyed – or possibly even fully formed – a cohesive and convincing narrative of what playwork is for, what it can do for children, or why this should be important to society.

Coming from two such leading lights, men who had each done so much to define playwork as an emerging profession,[5] this was a sobering reflection. When not debating the relative merits of evolutionary, developmental and socio-cultural perspectives on play, much of the two-day event was spent considering this credibility gap. Others at the meeting in Sheffield, however, wondered whether the greater hindrance to playwork's survival might be not so much the lack of an agreed or convincing story to tell, as the absence of a proper vehicle through which to tell it.

Dating back to Lady Allen's pioneering work of the 1950s and 1960s, playwork, as it became known, was central to the broader movement for children's right to play in the UK that eventually led to the big policy advances of 1998–2008. Included in these were the establishment of a vocational training and qualifications framework and higher education courses in playwork, but in spite of this, there has not been a sustained practitioner body since the profession first began to emerge.

In England, the various national play bodies, culminating in Play England in 2006,[6] had seen themselves as advocates for children's right to play in its broadest sense, as defined by article 31 of the UN Convention of the Rights of the Child. Staffed provision was just one among several areas of public life and public services where advocates sought to influence change in favour of children's right to play (Play England, 2007).

Furthermore, until very recently, the national play agencies in England have tended to be part of larger organisations, with broader remits than children's play, such as the National Playing Fields Association or the National Children's Bureau (NCB). Even the development of a recognised training and qualifications framework – which many saw as the key to defining playwork as a profession – while relying heavily on input from playworkers (or playwork trainers and service managers), was led not by an emergent professional body but by an employer-led agency, Skillsactive, licenced by the government to standardise workforce development for the sports and outdoor leisure sectors.

An attempt in the 2000s to create a practitioner-led national body for playworkers – in part to give playworkers themselves a greater voice in this activity – was short-lived. The Playworkers Association, founded in 2002, discovered that what its members most needed from organised action was pressure for better terms and conditions. It consequently joined the Community and Youth Workers Union en masse. When CYWU merged with Unite the Union, this led to the creation of a playwork convenor there and the Union now campaigns against government cuts to playwork services and jobs.

Skillsactive (2013), for its part, has launched the Register of Playwork Professionals: to reassure parents: that 'staff are appropriately qualified'; to regulate their adherence to National Occupational Standards; and to ensure their maintenance of on-going professional development.

All things being equal, unionisation and a national register of qualified practitioners could each be seen as milestones in the progression of playwork towards better recognition; steps, perhaps, on the way to its full professional status. Yet, especially in the context of the scarcity of funding and the absence of policy or regulatory drivers for services, each of these developments must be considered in the context of the greater challenges: not how to accredit qualified playworkers, or secure them greater rewards, but how to make the case for their very existence.

This logically leads to another big question: who is best placed to make that case? Neither the professional register at Skillsactive, or the playwork membership at Unite the Union, are ultimately governed by practitioners (or advocates, or trainers) of playwork. One of the conundrums of the English play and playwork movement has been its failure to take control of its national vehicles and thus, ultimately, of its own destiny.

The Children's Play Council (CPC), which transformed into Play England with the injection of strategic lottery funding in 2006, was never an independent body, operating instead as an alliance of other agencies, convened and hosted by one of its original members, NCB. As CPC, and then Play England, became increasingly successful, NCB took ever-greater control. When Play England then asserted its independence, voting to become a separate charity in 2010 (whilst a £15m lottery grant, partially awarded for the purpose, still had a year to run), NCB resisted: fearing, no doubt, for its own future after losing several government contracts. It would be a further four years before a hugely diminished Play England was able to announce its full independence from NCB, the lottery millions dedicated to the creation of a strategic, long-term support and development infrastructure for sustainable play provision (Big Lottery Fund, 2006) long since dissipated.

When the Sheffield summit convened by Else and Hughes led to a series of open meetings to consult on the need for, and the viability of a potential 'new vehicle for playwork' (Voce, 2013), it is perhaps, then, no surprise that the first priority emerging from the discussions was for any new body to be 'fully independent of other agencies, owned by and accountable only to its members'. The need to agree and communicate a clear and cohesive narrative of playwork also featured highly, as did consistency with the established 'Playwork principles' (PPSG, 2005). But what the playwork community most seems to want from a national body is a representative, collective voice: raising the status of playwork, campaigning for it and influencing policy that would be conducive to its growth 95% of those responding to a survey by the steering group formed to develop the idea thought such a body were needed, while 96% said they would join it (Voce, 2015).

With such a mandate, albeit couched in some strong caveats – most particularly that any new body should add to and not undermine or compete with existing national bodies in any of the home nations – the work to create a vehicle for playwork continues. Unlike the years culminating in the Play Strategy of 2008, there is now no government (or indeed any other) funding for such a venture and the work is therefore slow, dependent upon the spare time of people working elsewhere. It is progressing, nevertheless, and there is a strong sense that if the lack of financial or infrastructure support is the early price to pay for independence, then it will be a price worth paying.

Leaving aside the embryonic development of a new, independent vehicle for playwork – a small, as yet barely flickering light amidst so much gloom – there is another, perhaps even more pertinent sense in which the state of playwork in 2015 may not be as fragile as the policy and services landscape would paint it. This has to do with the playworker's role as advocate for children's play and the influence that this has, which may now be seen far beyond the adventure playground, and in many places other than the UK.

Although playwork's origins go back several decades earlier, it was the UN Convention on the Rights of the Child (CRC) of 1989 that galvanised the movement to seek proper public support for its work: to pressurise government bodies to act and make resources available. According to the UN itself, the CRC 'marked the transition from addressing children's immediate needs through charity alone … towards advocacy (for) systemic change for the realisation of (their) rights'. The 'Playwork principles' demand that playworkers, as well as making space and supporting children in their play, also 'act as advocates for play when engaging with adult led agendas'. They assert that 'the primacy of the play process should inform this advocacy in the policy, strategy and training arenas.'

This advocacy work by the playwork community is a consistent and important thread throughout the development of play policy, not just in the UK but internationally. The distinguished academic of children's rights and children's geographies, Professor Roger Hart (2015, p. xv), describes playwork as the 'uniquely British profession that understands children's daily lives out of school – their play, their culture and the spaces that best afford it – better than any other'. Who better than playworkers, then, to advocate for children's right to play?

It is no accident that much of the work leading to the UN's General Comment on Article 31 (Committee on the Rights of the Child [CRC], 2013) was done by British academics (Lester & Russell, 2010), steeped in the playwork tradition. Playwork is currently inspiring a revitalised play movement in the USA (Leichter-Saxby & Law, 2015) and Australia (Armitage, 2015). Playwork projects are having an impact in troubled places of the world as diverse as Romania (Brown) and Iran (Milne, 2015); and seeds are being sown across several Eastern European countries through the Volunteers in Playwork (VIPER, 2015) project of the University of Gloucestershire's Playwork Partnerships,

Closer to home, the pioneering legislation of the Welsh Government, placing a statutory duty on local authorities to assess and provide a sufficiency of play opportunities for their children, is relying to a large extent for its implementation and evaluation on methodologies and criteria developed by the playwork community, which, as in England, was also at the heart of the campaign to secure the policy that made it possible.

The playwork voice is an alternative one to the 'dominant discourse,' (Lester & Russell, 2008) wherein improving the child's future life chances, as measured through long-term projections of her earning capacity or health and disease patterns, is considered the primary, sometimes the sole, objective of child policy, whilst the child's ever-present, deeply instinctive desire to be freely expressed, to 'play and to dream' (McKelway, 1913) is at best trivialised, at worst conceived as a pathology.

Our experience as a community of practitioner-advocates working within (or 'under the aegis') of organisations happily aligned to that prevailing paradigm is perhaps analogous to the experience of many children. We owe it to them, and to ourselves, to champion the alternative; and, if we can maintain, as we should, a perspective on the current challenges that places them within the context of a global downturn and a political response to it that is depriving whole swathes of the public and voluntary sectors of oxygen – not just us – we may find that when there is again sufficient air to breathe, the world will be more receptive to our cause than it has ever been.

Disclosure statement

No potential conflict of interest was reported by the author.

Notes

1. The 'state' in this case is England, for which child policy resides with the UK government. The devolved governments of Scotland, Wales and Northern Ireland each have their own defined responsibilities for education and other children's services and have variously evolved different policies for play to that of the government in England.
2. Perry Else broadly defined good play provision by the 'Three Frees': (1) it is free of charge; (2) it offers freedom of choice; and (3) children are free to come and go. The Big Lottery Fund adopted these rules of thumb as the headline criteria for eligibility under its Children's Play Programme in England (2006–2011).

3. Uncalled for by the playwork community or by Play England, which led the lobby and would have pre-ferred a more gradual period of investment based on the pathfinder pilot studies of how best to adopt new design criteria (Shackell, Butler, Doyle, & Ball, 2008), the first phase of the strategy included £1m for every top-tier authority in England to build a total of 3500 new play areas by 2010–2011. The scale – and timescale – of this capital investment, the Playbuilder Programme, as well as itself being rather too hurried to allow for the innovation that was called for, also tended to overshadow other, arguably more important, strategic elements such as the Playshaper Programme, which aimed to embed play principles within planning, traffic, housing and other key local authority functions.

4. A closer reading reveals that this figure is derived from the only 32 councils who responded to a Freedom of Information request – and of these three had reduced their play spending to zero. A more accurate figure for the reduced spending on play – including all those authorities who presumably do not even have anyone left to field the enquiry – is therefore likely to be considerably higher

5. See, for example, Hughes' *Evolutionary playwork* (2001).

6. Play England, like its predecessor, the Children's Play Council, was not, in fact, an independent charity but operated 'under the aegis' of the National Children's Bureau until 2014, when it finally acquired full independent status.

References

Armitage, (2015). http://www.malarkeyon.com.au/marc-armitage-tour-schedule

Big Lottery Fund. (2006). *Children's play initiative*. Retrieved September 20, 2015, from https://www.biglotteryfund.org.uk/global-content/programmes/england/childrens-play

Brown, F., & Taylor, C. (Eds.). (2008). *Foundations of playwork*. Maidenhead: Open University Press.

Children's Play Policy Forum (CPPF). (2015). *4 asks for play* (campaigning pamphlet). London: CPPF.

Children's Rights Alliance for England (CRAE). (2015). *UK implementation of the convention on the rights of the child: Civil society alternative report to the committee on the rights of the child, England*. London: CRAE.

Cole-Hamilton, I., & Gill, T. (2002). *Making the case for play*. London: Children's Play Council.

Committee on the Rights of the Child (CRC). (2013). *Article 31: General comment No. 17 on the right of the child to rest, leisure, play, recreational activities, cultural life and the arts, adopted 17 April 2013*. Retrieved September 20, 2015, from http://www.iccp-play.org/documents/news/UNGC17.pdf

Department for Children, Schools and Families (DCSF). (2007). *The children's plan: Building brighter futures*. London: Stationery Office.

Department for Children, Schools and Families (DCSF). (2010). *Embedding the play strategy*. London: Crown Copyright.

Department for Children, Schools and Families (DCSF)/Department for Culture, Media and Sport (DCMS). (2008). *The play strategy*. London: Crown Copyright.

Hart, R. (2015). Foreword. In Voce, A. (Ed.), *Policy for play* (pp. xv–xvi). Bristol: Policy Press.

HM Treasury. (2003). *Every child matters*. London: Crown Copyright.

Hughes, B., (2001). *Evolutionary playwork and reflective analytic practice*, London: Routledge.

Leichter-Saxby, M., & Law, S. (2015). *The new adventure playground movement: How communities across the USA are returning risk and freedom to childhood*. Retrieved September 20, 2015, from http://popupadventureplay.blogspot.co.uk/2015/04/the-new-adventure-playground-movement.html

Lester, S., & Russell, W. (2008). *Play for a change, play, policy and practice: A review of contemporary perspectives*. London: Play England.

Lester, S., & Russell, W. (2010). *Children's right to play: An examination of the importance of play in the lives of children worldwide* (Working Paper No. 57). The Hague: Bernard van Leer Foundation.

McKelway, A. (1913). Declaration of dependence by the children of America in mines and factories and workshops assembled. In H. D. Hindman (Ed.), *Child labor: An American history (*2002*)* (p. 44). New York, NY: M.E. Sharpe.

Milne, J. (2015). An adventure playground for Halabja. *Journal of Playwork Practice, 1*(2), 229–231.

Play England. (2007). *Charter for children's play.* London: NCB. Retrieved from: http://www.playengland. org.uk/media/71062/charter-for-childrens-play.pdf

PPSG. (2005). *Playwork principles*, held in trust as honest brokers for the profession by the Playwork Principles Scrutiny Group. Retrieved September 20, 2015, from http://www.playwales.org.uk/eng/ playworkprinciples

Shackell, A., Butler, N., Doyle, P., & Ball, D. (2008). *Design for play: A guide to creating successful play spaces*, London: DCSF/Play England.

Skillsactive. (2013). http://www.playworkregister.org

VIPER, (2015). http://www.viperproject.eu

Voce, A. (2008). The state of play in England. In F. Brown, & C. Taylor (Eds.), *Foundations of playwork* (pp. 22–25). Maidenhead: Open University Press.

Voce, A. (2013). *Does playwork need a new vehicle?* Retrieved September 20, 2015, from Policy for Play [Internet blog] http://policyforplay.com/2014/01/10/does-playwork-need-a-new-vehicle/

Voce, A. (2015). *Playwork community says 'yes' to new vehicle.* Retrieved September 20, 2015, from Policy for Play [Internet blog] http://policyforplay.com/2015/03/10/playwork-community-says-yes-to-new-vehicle/

Memories of and reflections on play

Tracy R. Gleason

I lived as much of my childhood as possible outside of the here-and-now, in a time and place I can only describe as Elsewhere. It was a place that was simultaneously separate from and yet part of the real world, giving me whatever I thought I lacked – superpowers, wisdom, life experience, plucky sidekicks, children to nurture and protect, or situations that elicited the bravery I was unsure I truly possessed. On those occasions when my imagination successfully blocked out the pedantic or even painful aspects of reality, pretend play was the portal to maximum joy, a transcendent state of mind.

Inhabiting pretense creates a dream-like state, in which objects, events, and people can either be embraced or ignored according to the designs of the play. A pencil is a pencil for the pretend Teacher who is writing math problems for her students, but it can just as easily be a pirate's dagger or a fugitive's key for escaping prison. I was captivated by this power of transformation and how easily it could be communicated to my play partners. As in improvisational theater, a good partner would always accept one's suggestions, until the pretend world under construction took on a life of its own and began to exist with minimal effort because so much was understood. For me, this thrill of existing within the limitlessness of fantasy was matched only by the crush of the return to reality. At the time I could not name the unpleasant feeling that accompanied this return, but now I recognize it as a combination of frustration and grief. Shared fantasy took time to build – would we have the time, space, and ability to recapture it? Worst of all, the departure from Elsewhere forced me to acknowledge that it was not real. I yearned to return immediately, the way an addict misses a drug.

My earliest partner in pretense was my sister, Jennifer, three years older. According to my mother, my earliest pronunciation of her name was 'Funifer', a moniker appropriate for the person who introduced me to the joys of pretend when I was not quite two. We played an unsophisticated game that involved me ringing a doorbell – some toy that happened to have a bell on it – to gain entry into her bedroom, which was, of course, her residence. When she heard the bell, she would answer the door and welcome me in for tea or a chat. Then I would depart, only to ring again moments later. This script provided our tiny selves with a sense of power and a glimpse into the mysteries of adult behavior. We felt domestically invincible. Gradually, in tandem with our cognitive and social skills, our scripts became more complex. They began to include roles outside of our immediate experience and travel on all manner of cars, boats, and spaceships – all from the safety of home.

When other children joined my sister and me in our games, their ideas offered delightful expansions on the scripts we had developed between ourselves. Slight differences in lived experience and interests introduced exciting new storylines. Yet, the balance of these play sessions was usually uneven, because the time needed to establish the parameters lasted longer than the time spent playing. As sisters, our mutual experience allowed an unspoken understanding of how the games should proceed, and our coordination was effortless. A friend, however, might not share our assumptions, so that the thrill of a new infusion of ideas was tempered by the valuable minutes of playtime squandered in the interest of negotiation and compromise.

In middle childhood, we lived in a house that backed up into a small wood, in a neighborhood full of children our ages. In pairs, trios, and sometimes large, mixed-sex groups, we spent our summers and many afternoons after school roaming the woods, building houses out of sticks, jumping over creeks, torturing frogs, and playing games involving battles, pioneer living, or tragic, orphaned children surviving on their own in the wild, usually on the run from evil grown-ups. We invented crises to manage, threats to escape, and delightful discoveries of treasure or magical objects. The woods themselves were populated with all manner of people – mostly invisible – some enemies, some friends, and some magical. Some were rumored to be real, like a motorcycle gang that periodically roared through the woods and might run over an unfortunate child. We would play some games for days or weeks at a time, others for only a few hours. Those that lasted always involved compelling and elaborate invented worlds, in which fantasy intersected with reality in such a way that each child could mold the play to appeal to all involved. Those that did not last were killed by unappealing plots, uncooperative players, or conflicts that could not be resolved. Regardless, while it lasted, there in the woods time would stop, and all that existed were the stone tools and stick shelters we had created ourselves, using the skills, smarts, and powers associated with our pretend identities.

In the dead of winter, when the woods were too cold or muddy for us to enjoy for long periods, my playmates and I transferred our activities indoors using dress up clothes, puppets, dolls, and Barbies. Early in childhood, we had all discovered that thoughts and feelings could be projected onto inanimate objects, and of course our own relationships were replicated between them. Like many children, I would worry that a stuffed elephant had grown sad if neglected for too long, and imagine that new doll was shy when meeting the family. These projections were even transferred to objects without animate form. My toy telephone liked to be close to the xylophone in the toy box since they had become friends based on their mutual ability to make lovely chiming sounds. And when pressured to give up the infant toys, I could sense the feelings of betrayal emanating from my stacking rings and jack-in-the-box, and I was genuinely sorry.

Today, as a professor at Wellesley College and a researcher of social processes and relationships in preschool-aged children, I have spent hours interviewing small people about their invisible imaginary companions and objects that they personify and animate into relationship partners. Some children are enthusiastic about answering my questions, delighting in my interest in their play. Others answer shyly, maybe even reluctantly at first, and remind me that their invisible friends are not real. When they do so, however, they often whisper, hoping the companion will not overhear. I understand this compulsion. To confess in a regular voice, their knowledge that the imaginary companion is entirely pretend would shatter the precious bubble that surrounds their creations, allowing them to travel freely within reality, much like a space suit on the moon. Acknowledging play as such kills the capacity to experience it emotionally as reality. As adults, we engage in the same process when we choose to either feel the devastation of a beloved character's death in a film or remind ourselves that it is 'just a movie' so that we can remain unmoved.

Engaging in these social forms of imagination as a child and then investigating them as an adult has highlighted several ideas for me. One is that the pinnacle of imaginative play is a level of involvement and focus that transcends time and place – indeed, imagination is defined as a transfer of mind outside of the here-and-now. Individuals who develop and fine-tune this transfer of mind in play acquire a sort of expertise that allows them to simultaneously exist in the real world and pull useful aspects of Elsewhere into it. Fiction writers achieve this duality when their characters come alive and direct their own stories (Taylor, Hodges, & Kohanyi, 2003; Watkins, 2000), and creativity is often described as an ability to harness absurd thoughts and unlikely connections in the creation of something new (Mumford, 2003). Imagination gives us access to ideas we did not know we had, as when imagined conversations with real others help us solve problems that have perplexed us for days or regulate emotions that feel out of control (Gleason, Tarmidi, & Jeong, 2014; Honeycutt, Zagacki, & Edwards, 1990). My own theoretical snags are often best addressed by imagined conversations with my graduate school mentors as I stare out of my office window.

Another remarkable aspect of imagination is just how early we begin to develop this expertise. Even toddlers follow the pretense stipulations and transformations associated with pouring tea from a toy tea pot, acknowledging on some level that Elsewhere exists (Harris, Kavanaugh, Wellman, & Hickling, 1993). By preschool, children can reliably identify when others have entered a pretense scenario (Richert & Lillard, 2004). These simple abilities turn out to be useful for our psychological functioning. The concept that a world of thoughts, emotions, and actions could exist outside of that which is immediately available to our senses enables all of the mental work we do in trying to understand others. Cognitive tasks critical to successful social interaction, such as theory of mind, rely on imagination to consider what another person might be thinking.

The idea that imagination is implicated in our real social interactions is perhaps the most important. After all, interactions are the basis of relationships, and ties to others are central to human life (Reis, Collins, & Berscheid, 2000). We are, fundamentally, social creatures, meaning that the tendency of some of us to extend our social concerns to the emotional state of the jack-in-the-box is understandable. We anthropomorphize, invoke the presence of deities, and imagine ourselves in close relationships with celebrities when we feel our real human con-nections are lacking or we are unclear of our social identities (Epley, Waytz, & Cacioppo, 2007; Giles, 2002). These uses of imagination help us rehearse and plan for real interactions that might be conflict-ridden or otherwise emotionally laden (Honeycutt et al., 1990). Imagination facilitates all of those functions that help us relate to each other every day, such as perspective-taking, empathy, morality, and kindness. Harnessing imagination in service of these social tasks began for me with a fake doorbell. My hours spent negotiating storylines translate into sat-isfactory compromises in committee meetings, and my childhood concerns for my new doll's feel-ings facilitated my empathy for my children on the first day of kindergarten.

As a researcher of imagination, I worry that the time and space currently allocated in our schools and homes for developing imagination is insufficient to foster the skills children will need as they become adults. Rather than obsessing over reading comprehension or math problem-solving strategies, I fret about whether recess is long enough to afford young children a satisfying trip to Elsewhere. I wonder whether the use of educational iPad applications instead of peer tutoring is interfering with their education more than it broadens their imaginative horizons. And like all parents, I seek to recreate for my nine-year-old twins the aspects of my own childhood that were most precious to me. Consequently, my house has a bin from which all manner of dress up clothes is constantly exploding, shelves full of fiction, and in the absence of nearby woods, a wonky-shaped tree house in the yard. Since the birth of my children, I have religiously and militantly tried to find time every day in which they can choose their own adventures, with each other or with other children, but without me or other directive adults. In this quest, I have found like-minded others, but we often feel we are swimming upstream in the current zeitgeist of academic assessment.

Recently, a small incident assuaged some of my anxiety that imagination is getting short shrift in my children's development. One night, as I cuddled my daughter at bedtime, she suddenly pulled away and sat straight up with some urgency, as though she had just remembered some critical task. Gently, one by one, she picked up each of the many stuffed animals strewn around her bed. She did not speak, but paused to look deeply into each set of embroidered, felt, or button eyes, communicating telepathically her good night wishes. She kissed each soft head and arranged all but the favorite into carefully designated sleeping spots in a long row at the edge of her bed. Then, cuddling the most precious in her arms, she lay back down and went to sleep.

Disclosure statement

No potential conflict of interest was reported by the author.

References

Epley, N., Waytz, A., & Cacioppo, J. T. (2007). On seeing human: A three-factor theory of anthropomorphism. *Psychological Review, 114*, 864–886.

Giles, D. C. (2002). Parasocial interaction: A review of the literature and a model for future research. *Media Psychology, 4*, 279–305.

Gleason, T., Tarmidi, K., & Jeong, J. (2014). *Imagined interactions promote complex solutions to hypothetical social dilemmas*. Paper presented at the annual meeting of the Association for Psychological Science, San Francisco, CA.

Harris, P. L., Kavanaugh, R. D., Wellman, H. M., & Hickling, A. K. (1993). Young children's understanding of pretense. *Monographs of the Society for Research in Child Development, 58*, i+iii+v+1–107. doi:10.2307/1166074.

Honeycutt, J. M., Zagacki, K. S., & Edwards, R. (1990). Imagined interaction and interpersonal communication. *Communication Reports, 3*, 1–8.

Mumford, M. D. (2003). Where have we been, where are we going? Taking stock in creativity research. *Creativity Research Journal, 15*, 107–120.

Reis, H., Collins, W. A., & Berscheid, E. (2000). The relationship context of human behavior and development. *Psychological Bulletin, 126*, 844–872.

Richert, R. A., & Lillard, A. S. (2004). Observers' proficiency at identifying pretense acts based on behavioral cues. *Cognitive Development, 19*, 223–240.

Taylor, M., Hodges, S., & Kohanyi, A. (2003). The illusion of independent agency: Do adult fiction writers experience their characters as having minds of their own? *Imagination, Cognition, and Personality, 22*, 361–380.

Watkins, M. (2000). *Invisible guests: The development of imaginal dialogues* (3rd ed.). Woodstock, CT: Spring.

Best of times to worst of times? Appraising the changing landscape of play in the UK

The following 10 papers were first presented at a conference in Leicester (in the UK), on 22 May 2013. The conference, which was convened by the Geographies of Children, Youth and Families Research Group of the Royal Geographical Society (with IBG), brought together play providers, practitioners and researchers to discuss the prospects for play in 2013 and beyond. The title of the conference was *Play in Times of Austerity*.

INTRODUCTION

Complex geographies of play provision dis/investment across the UK

John H. McKendrick, Peter Kraftl, Sarah Mills, Stefanie Gregorius and Grace Sykes

This introductory paper sets the context for a collection of 10 papers examining, *Best of times to worst of times? Appraising the changing landscape of play in the UK*. It is argued that the contemporary geography of play investment in the UK is complex, with dis/investment in much of England being contrasted with much stronger national commitments to play in the devolved administrations of Scotland and Wales. However, even in devolved UK, Austerity pressures on local government budgets have rendered it difficult to sustain, let alone scale up, inherited levels of spending on play services. Through austerity, the national narrative of play that was fostered in the early years of the Millennium is also being challenged by a commitment to localism. The paper ends by introducing the four themes that are addressed in the collection, i.e. 'how did we get here'; 'austerity'; 'austerity as threat'; 'austerity as opportunity'; and 'rethinking play and society'.

Introduction

Wyatt loses his house in Wyoming, beatrice loses her park in Battersea

The unravelling of the US housing market in late 2006 triggered a series of events that have had far-reaching consequences not only for the global economy, but also for children's play and playwork in the UK. In the aftermath of the Global Recession of 2009, the UK elected a new Government in 2010, which immediately implemented an 'austerity programme', seeking to reduce the Government budget deficit. Within 3 months, notice had been served of cuts to play provision in England Play England (2011). The Education Secretary wrote to local authorities advising them not to utilise unspent monies that had been allocated to them under the previous administration's *Playbuilder* programme (DCSF & DCMS, 2008), unless there was clear evidence of a contractual arrangement to progress construction (Vasagar, 2010). The unravelling of the transformation that was envisaged of England's play landscape was cemented in October of that year when the Minister again wrote to Directors of Children's Services in English local authorities to advise them of the 'saving' of £20.8 million of the £75 million that had been allocated for play capital budget spend in 2010–2011 (Gove, 2010). Furthermore, less overt cuts to play funding were to follow. These cuts can be understood in the wider context of disproportionate cuts, through UK Government spending reviews, to public services for children and young people (CIPFA, 2011) and to consequent increases in levels of child poverty and deprivation (CRAE, 2013).

As it is not a statutory service, play is particularly vulnerable to secondary cuts, i.e. local cut-backs to service provision that, in this instance, were a consequence of the UK Government reducing the budgets of local Government by 7% per annum from 2010 to 2014 (HM Treasury, 2010). As local Government struggles to fulfil its statutory obligations, severe cuts to non-statutory services such as play have followed. In some authorities this has been achieved through outsourcing of service. In the London Borough of Camden, for instance, it is not clear how many of the 200 playworkers who lost their jobs have been absorbed by the community-led service that now delivers play locally (Morton, 2012a; 2012b). What can be said with certainty is that the reconfiguration of the playground in Battersea Park in the London Borough of Wandsworth from a renowned open-access adventure playground to one with fixed equipment in landscaped grounds was one that was not welcomed by the local community (The Spectacle Blog, 2013) and play professionals alike (Hocker, 2014). Furthermore, it should be noted that children, who are arguably most affected by these developments, hardly have a voice in the political decision-making process (Bosco, 2010).

The Leicester seminar: **Playwork in Times of Austerity**

In May of 2013, the Geographies of Children, Youth and Families Research Group of the Royal Geographical Society (with IBG) organised a one-day seminar at the University of Leicester to discuss the issue of *Playwork in Times of Austerity.* The idea behind the event was to provide a forum in which academic geographers and playwork practitioners could consider the issues and responses to what was pre-conceived as a contemporary 'crisis' for play in the UK. In addition to Mick Conway, the keynote speaker, ruminating on a long and distinguished playwork career (Conway, 2014), the deliberations comprised two sets of three formal papers to the themes of 'cuts in focus' and 'rethinking what matters', wrapped around a Pecha Kucha session of nine mini-presentations, which provided concise and focused commentary on very specific aspects of 'play and austerity'.

In terms of the academic geographers who attended, the seminar was situated particularly within cross-disciplinary research on children's everyday spaces, places and movements. Within academic geography, this research has come to be known as 'Children's Geographies', although, like the journal of the same name, this work encapsulates work by geographers, anthropologists, sociologists and others (Kraftl, Horton, & Tucker, 2012). Research on Children's Geographies has several affinities with that on play and playwork. On the one hand, it emphasises the diverse everyday experiences of children in their localities – especially in outdoor spaces – and the ways in which they negotiate adult-imposed regulations (e.g. Holt, 2011). On the other hand, such research has examined how space and place – especially institutions like schools – are central to the construction of contemporary notions of childhood, on which many assumptions about the parameters of children's play are founded (e.g. Holloway & Valentine, 2000; Holloway, Hubbard, Joens, Pimlott-Wilson, & Jons, 2010).

This collection in the *International Journal of Play* brings together ten of the papers from the Leicester seminar, each of which focused on the broader implications for play in UK society (a smaller collection, which focused on issues for playwork practitioners, was published in the *Journal of Playwork Practice* – McKendrick, Horton, Kraftl, & Else, 2014). Four themes are addressed in this collection, i.e. 'how did we get here'; 'austerity as threat'; 'austerity as opportunity' and 'rethinking play and society'. In thinking through the significance for play of 'the era of austerity', it is important to acknowledge that there are other significant and recent developments that may help understand the ways in which austerity has impacted on play in the UK, two of which are now introduced.

The construction and consumption of the national narrative for play in the UK

The play and playwork sector in the UK has presented a convincing and wide-ranging case for investing in play. As Tim Gill explains in more detail in the opening paper in this collection, the years around the Millennium were ones in which the play sector was challenged to articulate the value of play (Playlink, NPFA and Children's Play Council, 2000), which in turn, led to unprecedented levels of national investment in children's play by the UK Government and other national bodies (Department of Culture, Media and Sports, 2004).

A strong narrative from the UK play sector in recent years has been that play is about more than play. It has been argued with conviction that play can make a positive contribution to achieving a wide range of socially desirable goals. For example, among other virtues, play is promoted as a means through which children's learning can be enhanced (Scottish Government, n.d.; Kraftl, 2013), obesity can be tackled (National Toy Council, n.d.), and social inclusion can be promoted (Playboard NI, n.d.; Skelton, 2009). Such acknowledgments resonate with Children's Geographies research, which has examined the challenges and opportunities facing children's play in diverse geographical contexts.

The diffusion of the case for play is also evident in the proliferation of advice that has been generated to facilitate play in different settings; these have been underpinned by evidence-based reviews. For example, Play Scotland and CPIS have published a range of factsheets that provide guidance on how to facilitate play in a wide range of environments including institutional settings (schools and hospitals), social settings (intergenerational play and playtime) and environmental settings (natural environments, sand play and wooded areas) (CPIS, nd; Play Scotland, n.d.).

On the other hand, play is also promoted as a whole, as well as for its parts. A fundamental tenet of the sector's play principles is acknowledgment of the value of play for its own sake (Skillsactive, n.d.). The *Playwork Principles* are not alone in promoting play *per se*; most definitions of play in the UK, and all of those that originate from within the play sector, make reference to play being 'freely chosen', 'personally driven' and 'intrinsically motivated' (e.g. Russell & Lester, 2008).

Although the UK play sector has risen to the challenge of articulating the value of play, it is less clear how this message has been received. While others (especially Early Years Educators) welcomed the acknowledgement of the contribution that play makes to achieving their goals, it is less clear whether the inherent value of play is a message that has been as warmly welcomed by those outside the play profession. Indeed, the same Minister for Education who initiated the play cuts in 2010, demonstrated an alarming misunderstanding of the value of play in the Autumn of 2013 in recalling an ancedote from schools in Kent. In a speech in which he acknowledged the importance of teaching, he reported that,

Some schools have been pressured to fit in with prevailing doctrines, even against their own instincts. Some nurseries and schools in Kent, for example, reported to us that … [they] were told that children were not allowed to tidy up, or be asked to put their coats on, in case it interrupted 'child-initiated play'. (Gove, 2013)

Setting aside the gross misrepresentation of child-initiated play that this represents, that a Government minister considers that there is political capital to be gained by ridiculing children's play in such a fashion should be troubling to the play sector in the UK, as it suggests that there is a wider public that would be receptive to such a message.

Changing play: the role of the local state and the emergence of the devolved national region in lean times

As the examples from London in the opening section of this paper suggest, the political geographies of play in the UK are not stable. On the contrary, the role of the state in relation to play is ridden with tensions between the opposing forces of centralisation and de-centralisation (Hulme, McKay, & Cracknell, 2013).

Playgrounds and play spaces are more than merely sites for play: the geographies of play matter across a variety of scales. Gagen (2000) demonstrates how the development of municipal playgrounds in US cities in the early twentieth century reflected the concerns of social reformers to shape child development, in order to produce 'American' identities that were both gendered and racialised. Through time, the provision of play spaces extended beyond showpiece provision and such national ideals, and was woven into the fabric of neighbourhoods at a more local scale. As Cunningham and Jones (1999) outline, town planners were at the fore in promoting such formal play space in the residential environments that they were creating in the mid-late twentieth century. On the other hand, playgrounds are not merely provided by the local state or by other interest groups *for* communities; campaigning for, and the construction of, neighbourhood playgrounds is also a grassroots activity led by community groups who desire these spaces (Hetherington, 1999). Thus, by the end of the twentieth century, it was widely accepted that playground playspace should be available where children were expected to play, i.e. in residential environments and municipal parks.

The public provision of playspace by the local state in the UK was politicised when local government expenditure contracted in the 1970s and 1980s. This coincided with the development of a national consciousness for play, as national and regional collectives of play workers developed from the grassroots. Once the recipient of playspace, communities, aligned with playworkers, were now agitating against the local state to protect their community resource.

The development of a UK national frame of reference for play fractured in the 1990s with the introduction of Devolution. Play was within the remit of the new Devolved Administrations in Scotland, Wales and Northern Ireland, while the UK Government retained responsibility for play in England. Different devolution pathways for play followed, leading to a distinct spatial patternings of play at the sub-national level in the UK. In England, the central state adopted a prominent role, directing and directly funding significant investment in play infrastructure. A strong Play England emerged, as did strong regional associations for play in England. Play also developed in the devolved national regions in the 1990s, but on a much smaller scale and at a much slower pace. All three of the national play associations in devolved UK strengthened (Play Scotland, Play Wales and Playboard NI) and there were some significant national commitments to play in Wales, such as in 2002 when Wales became the first country in the world to adopt a national play policy (Play Wales, n.d., a). However, on the whole, the scale of investment was much more modest in Scotland, Wales and Northern Ireland, when compared to England.

As noted above, a change of UK government in 2010 heralded the introduction of a 'politics of austerity', through which an opportunity was provided for the new Government to further its ideological commitment to a 'smaller' central state. Consequently, the UK state has adopted a less prominent role in funding play. The Department for Education, which had (as the Department for Children, Schools and Families) led government initiatives on play in England, stated in April 2011 that 'full responsibility for play will be returned to local authorities and their communities' (Burlington, 2011). It is not without consequence, that this scalar shift in the responsibility for play from central to local government coincides with a significant reduction in the monies available to local government.

This 'return' to localism in play provision in England contrasts with the situation in Wales, Scotland and Northern Ireland, where national governments have adopted a more prominent role in supporting play. The Scottish Government introduced Scotland's first National Play Strategy in 2013 (Scottish Government, 2013); a Play Sufficiency Duty came into force in Wales in November 2012 as part of their anti-poverty drive (Section 11 of the *Children and Families (Wales) Measure 2010* – Play Wales, n.d., b); and the NI Executive endorsed a Play and Leisure Strategy and Implementation Plan for Northern Ireland in March 2011 (OFMDFM, 2011). Even here, the political geography is complex, with the national state investing in play at a time when, as in England, the local state is finding it more difficult to continue supporting it.

Introduction to this collection

The papers in this edited collection are organised into four themes, each of which comprises two papers. The opening theme – *How We Got Here* – presents insider and outsider accounts of the recent history of play investment in England. In this first, Tim Gill, one of the UK's leading thinkers on contemporary childhood and a highly respected and leading figure in the UK play sector for several decades (e.g. Gill, 2007), shares his thoughts from when he was seconded in 2002 to the then Department for Culture, Media and Sport from his position as Director of the Children's Play Council (now Play England) to lead the first ever UK Government sponsored review of children's play. Tim makes it clear that play in England is shaped by the wider society of which it is part; both benefitting from opportunities presented, and now suffering from constraints that it imposes. In the second paper, insights from the 'back end' of this era of investment are provided by Alexandra Long, Senior Lecturer in Playwork at Leeds Metropolitan University. Having worked as a Play Manager in Bradford (North Yorkshire) and Camden (London) throughout the 2000s, Alexandra reflects on the legacy of the Big Lottery programme evaluation, which followed the investment of £123 million in England between 2006 and 2012 (Smith & Day, 2011). Alexandra fears for the consequences of the play sector not embracing its own 'objectives for play provision' as a framework to evidence the value of investment in play in times of austerity (and beyond).

Austerity as threat, the second theme, also comprises two complementary papers. Helen Woolley, Reader in Landscape Architecture and Society at the University of Sheffield, explores the nature and implication of austerity cuts in the city of Sheffield, a city of half a million people in the north of England. Helen finds little comfort in the way in which the city is responding to the cuts, with retraction of provision to be found in many forms. John McKendrick (Board of Directors of Play Scotland and Glasgow Caledonian University) and Chris Martin (UNITE Union's Playwork Convenor) then provide an overview of the cuts in Scotland and SW England, two parts of the UK with contrasting play trajectories in recent times. They identify limitations in speaking 'collectively' about play and playwork in the UK, as they explore the extent to which the wider funding context for play services is reflected in play practitioners' reflections on their experiences in 2013.

The third theme, *Austerity as Opportunity,* considers the possibility that austerity need not (only) be problematic. For Alice Ferguson (Director of Playing Out) and Angie Page (University of Bristol) the disinvestment from provision of formal public playspace affords opportunities for communities to rediscover their streets as play spaces. Presenting both an insider and outsider perspective, this paper extols the value of street play for its potential to transform both the everyday residential environment and children's physical health. Rob Wheway (Children's Play Information Service) is also supportive of outdoor play. However, rather than seek the organised grassroots creation of street playspace, he seeks to champion the cause of 'free play'. Rob's argument is grounded on a career's worth of field observations in which it is consistently demonstrated that children travel only very short distances to access neighbourhood play.

Rethinking Play and Society is the final theme. Arthur Battram (Plexity) argues that there is a need to rethink the general orientation of play in the UK and the tendency to posit play futures as a straight choice of between strategic playwork and environmental playwork. Arthur articulates a 'third way' for play, one which is less concerned with infrastructure (or accessing that infrastructure) and is primarily concerned to engender a culture that is more supportive of play. Finally, Cindy Regaldo, (*University College London*) articulates the case that playfulness is a fruitful strategy to deploy in advancing 'publicly initiated scientific research'. Here, a wider role for play is envisaged that is integral to progressive grassroots community development action.

Finally, the authors of this editorial return in conclusion to summarise the key points. We identify six overarching themes to emerge across the papers and consider the significance for the future of play in the UK, and beyond.

Disclosure statement

No potential conflict of interest was reported by the authors.

References

Bosco, F. J. (2010). Play, work or activism? Broadening the connections between political and children's geographies. *Children's Geographies, 8*(4), 381–390.

Burlington, S. (2011). *Letter to Eleanor Thompson*, 4Children in responses to questions submitted to the Department for Education). April 6, 2011. Retrieved November 15, 2013, from http://www.4children. org.uk/Files/b7f98172–1fec-4ffa-b72b-a21c00c9932e/110406-Reply-to-APPG-on-Sure-Start-from-DfE.pdf.

Children's Play Information Service [CPIS]. (n.d.). *Factsheets*. Retrieved November 14, 2014, from http:// www.ncb.org.uk/cpis/resources/factsheets.

CIPFA. (2011). *Smart cuts? public spending on children's social care*. London: NSPCC.

CRAE Children's Rights Alliance for England [CRAE]. (2013). *State of children's rights in England: Review of government action on United Nations' recommendations for strenghthening children's rights in the UK*. London: Author.

Conway, M. (2014). The thin of it – surviving and thriving in austerity. *Journal of Playwork Practice, 1*(1), 87–91.

Cunningham, C. J., & Jones, M. A. (1999). The playground: A confession of failure? *Built Environment, 25* (1), 11–17.

DCMS. (2004). *Getting serious about play. A review of children's play*. London: TSO.

DCSF and DCMS. (2008). *The play strategy*. London: TSO.

Gagen, E. (2000). An example to us all: Child development and identity construction in early 20th-century playgrounds. *Environment and Planning A, 32*(4), 599–616.

Gill, T. (2007). *No fear: Growing up in a risk averse society*. London: Calouste Gulbenkian Foundation.

Gove, M. (2010). *Michael Gove's letter to directors of children's services*. October 20, 2010. Retrieved November 14, 2013, from https://www.gov.uk/government/publications/revised-play-capital-allocations-for-local-authorities.

Gove, M. (2013). *Michael Gove speaks about the importance of teaching*. September 13, 2013. Retrieved November 14, 2013, from https://www.gov.uk/government/speeches/michael-gove-speaks-about-the-importance-of-teaching.

Hetherington, S. (1999). Playgrounds as community landscapes. *Built Environment, 25*(1), 25–34.

Hocker, P. (2014). A play space to beat all. *Journal of Playwork Practice, 1*(1), 104–108.

Holloway, S., Hubbard, P., Joens, H. & Pimlott-Wilson, H. (2010). Geographies of education and the significance of children, youth and families. *Progress in Human Geography, 34*, 583–600.

Holloway, S., & Valentine, G. (2000). Spatiality and the new social studies of childhood. *Sociology, 34*(4), 763–783.

Holt, L. (2011). *Geographies of children, youth and families: International perspectives*. London: Routledge.

Hulme, R., McKay, J. & Cracknell, D. (2013). From commissar to auctioneer? The changing role of directors in managing children's services in a period of austerity. *Educational Management. Administration and Leadership, 43*, 77–91. doi:10.1177/1741143213494886.

HM Treasury. (2010). *Spending review 2010*. London: TSO. Retrieved November 14, 2013, from https:// www.gov.uk/government/uploads/system/uploads/attachment_data/file/203826/Spending_review_2010.pdf.

Kraftl, P. (2013). *Geographies of alternative education: Diverse learning spaces for children and young people*. Bristol: Policy Press.

Kraftl, P., Horton, J., & Tucker, F. (2012). *Critical geographies of childhood and youth: Contemporary policy and practice*. Bristol: Policy Press.

McKendrick, J., Horton, J., Kraftl, P., & Else, P. (2014). Space for playwork in times of austerity? *Journal of Playwork Practice, 1*(1), 79–118.

Morton, K. (2012a). Camden to close play services, *Nursery World*, January 18, 2012. Retrieved November 7, 2013, from http://www.nurseryworld.co.uk/article/1112784/camden-close-play-services?HAYILC=RELATED.

Morton, K. (2012b). Camden Council launches new play service, *Nursery World*, September 14, 2012. Retrieved November 7, 2013, from http://www.nurseryworld.co.uk/article/1150110/camden-council-launches-new-play-service?HAYILC=RELATEDNSPCC.

National Toy Council. (n.d.). *Active play and health*. London. Retrieved November 14, 2014, from http://www.btha.co.uk/wp-content/uploads/2012/10/active_play.pdf.

Office of the First Minister and Deputy First Minister. (2011). *Play and leisure implementation plan*. Belfast. Retrieved November 8, 2013, from http://www.northernireland.gov.uk/play_and_leisure_implementation_plan.pdf.

Playboard NI. (n.d.). *Play and social inclusion*. Belfast. Retrieved November 14, 2014, from http://www.playboard.org/Uploads/document/180820091434-2137642286.pdf.

PLAYLINK, NPFA and the Children's Play Council. (2000). *Best play: What play provision can do for children*. London: NPFA.

Play England. (2011). *Government to discontinue national play contracts*. February 14, 2011. Retrieved November 15, 2014, from http://www.playengland.org.uk/news/2011/02/government-to-discontinue-national-play-contracts.aspx.

Play Scotland. (n.d.). *Factsheets*. Retrieved November 14, 2014, from http://www.playscotland.org/resources/factsheets/.

Play Wales. (n.d., a). *Play Wales Timeline*. Retrieved November 15, 2014, from http://www.playwales.org.uk/login/uploaded/documents/INFORMATION%20SHEETS/play%20in%20wales%20timeline.pdf.

Play Wales. (n.d., b). *Play sufficiency*. Retrieved November 8, 2013, from http://www.playwales.org.uk/eng/sufficiency.

Russell, W., & Lester, S. (2008). *Play for a change: Play policy and practice. A review of contemporary perspectives*. London: Play England.

Scottish Government. (2013). *Play strategy for Scotland: Our vision*. Edinburgh. Retrieved November 8, 2013, from http://www.scotland.gov.uk/Resource/0042/00425722.pdf.

Scottish Government. (n.d.). *Play, talk, read*. Retrieved November 14, 2013, from http://www.playtalkread.org.

Skelton, T. (2009). Children's geographies/geographies of children: Play, work, mobilities and migration. *Geography Compass, 3*(4), 1430–1448.

Skillsactive. (n.d.). *Playwork principles*. Retrieved November 14, 2013, from http://www.skillsactive.com/our-sectors/playwork/playwork-principles.

Smith, N., & Day, L. (2011). *Children's play programme evaluation. Final report to big lottery fund*. Birmingham: Ecorys.

Spectacle Blog. (2013). *New playground in Battersea Park*. April 30, 2013. Retrieved November 14, 2013, from http://www.spectacle.co.uk/spectacleblog/tag/battersea-park-adventure-playground-2/.

Vasagar, J. (2010). Playground plans shelved under government spending cuts. *The Guardian*, August 11, 2010. Retrieved November 14, 2013, from http://www.theguardian.com/politics/2010/aug/11/playground-plans-frozen-spending-cuts.

HOW WE GOT HERE

Play in the good times: the (English) inside story

Tim Gill [ID]

In 2007 the UK government announced a National Play Strategy for England, along with £235 million of public expenditure to implement it. This followed an earlier government decision in 2001 to allocate £155 million of National Lottery funding to improving children's play opportunities. The funding was directed at public playgrounds, adventure playgrounds, playwork training, good practice guidance and local and national coordination and policy. This paper gives a personal account of the story behind this unprecedented degree of support for children's play, and offers some thoughts on how and why it came about. It draws on the experiences and observations of the author, who for a time worked closely with those making and carrying out the key decisions.

Writing this in late 2013, it is hard to believe that it has been only five years since the government announced a 10-year National Play Strategy for England (the first ever) – and what is more, committed £235 million to implementing it. I was in Parliament with other play advocates on the day the original spending announcement was made in 2007, and can still recall our amazement. We knew that a play strategy was in the pipeline, but had no idea the sums devoted to it would be so substantial.[1]

The English play sector has been on quite a rollercoaster ride in the last decade or so. This paper offers my personal perspective on this journey, as someone who for much of the period was close to the action. It is inevitably a partial account. But I have tried to make it objective, and to avoid too much political point-scoring.

First, some numbers. Table 1 gives figures for Government and National Lottery spending on children's play over four 3-year periods from 1997 to 2008. (Note that during this period, governments of the day had greater influence over the spending programmes of the National Lottery than they do now.)[2]

It was in 1994 that I joined the Children's Play Council (an alliance of charities and public bodies with an interest in children's play, which in 2006 became Play England), and I was its Director from 1997 to 2004. This gave me a fair impression of the status, in Government and Whitehall, of children's play, and of what might be called the play lobby (by which I mean those most actively engaged in advocating for play, at the national and local levels). In the late

Table 1. Government and National Lottery spending commitments, England/UK, 1997–2008.

Announcement date/s	Expenditure	Spending period	Description
1999	£1.2 million	1997–1999	Grant funding for Children's Play Council (now Play England), Children's Play Information Service and SPRITO (now Skillsactive)
2000	£10.8 million	2000–2005	National Lottery (New Opportunities Fund) 'Better Play' programme
2001	£155 million	2006–2011	National Lottery (Big Lottery Fund) Children's Play Initiative
2007	£235 million	2008–2011	Department for Children, Schools and Families Play Strategy

1990s, we had a minimal profile, and a reputation for being difficult to do business with. I recall one senior civil servant saying that dealing with the national play agencies was like herding cats. In 1998 Cabinet minister Chris Smith MP echoed this view in a speech at a play conference, at which he said that the sector needed to 'speak with one voice' if it wanted government to listen.[3]

As Secretary of State for Culture, Media and Sport, Chris Smith was well placed to develop the government's interest in play. His department not only held the lead role (such as it was) for the issue, it also led on government policy on the National Lottery. Moreover, Smith's own parliamentary constituency was in the London Borough of Islington, which was at the time one of the Councils that invested the most in play services, especially staffed adventure playgrounds (and this is still the case today).[4] Smith would have been familiar with the contribution that play provision makes to the lives of children, families and communities in his constituency.

In May 2001 Smith secured a manifesto commitment from the Labour Party to a £200 million National Lottery spending programme on children's play (made in the run-up to that year's general election). Devolution meant that the eventual figure for England was £155 million.[5]

The play strategy, when combined with the National Lottery funding, added up to unprecedented levels of investment in improving play opportunities for children. The shopping list for the £235 million play strategy included:

- 3500 new or improved public play spaces
- 30 new staffed adventure playgrounds in disadvantaged areas
- Training and staff development for 4000 playworkers
- A training programme aimed at 'helping the professionals who design and manage our neighbourhoods to understand the importance of play and child-friendly spaces'
- A new national performance indicator for local authorities
- New guidance on design, risk management and partnership working

Early indications suggested that this investment was having a dramatic impact on children's lives. An authoritative annual survey of children and young people's views found that, in the single year between 2008 and 2009, the satisfaction rating for parks and play areas in their area rose from 45% to 54%.[6]

Why did this growth in investment and interest in play between 1997 and 2008 happen? In particular, what led Government, over just a few years, to ramp up its own spending on play from virtually zero to hundreds of millions of pounds? Only those who were ministers and senior officials at the time can give definitive answers to these questions. But here are my thoughts.

The government's change in stance has to be seen in the light of the policy context at the time, and also the political context. Labour's first two terms were marked by rising investment in public services across the public sector, including those aimed at children and young people. In 2007 Gordon Brown replaced Tony Blair as Prime Minister, and Ed Balls became Secretary of State for the renamed Department for Children, Schools and Families. Along with the new name came a renewed commitment to breaking down the barriers between different services and disciplines, and that embraced wider goals around children's well-being. This shift – of which the play strategy was a key part – was given a further push by the publication of a UNICEF study of child well-being that placed the UK bottom of a 'league table' of 21 industrialised countries.[7]

Intriguingly, the play strategy announcement received little party political criticism at the time. If anything, the Conservative Party was vying with Labour in the battle to show who had the most coherent response to the UNICEF report, and the best ideas for improving children's well-being. In March 2007 – a month after the publication of that report – Tory leader David Cameron launched an inquiry into childhood. Announcing the initiative, shadow cabinet minister David Willetts was quoted in the *Guardian* newspaper (26 March 2007) as saying,

> Making friends, building relationships, experimenting, imagining, taking risks and making mistakes are important for the mental health and wellbeing of children. We have long warned about the dangers of red tape on business; we now need to worry about the red tape on childhood. We need to allow children to have vivid lives and everyday adventures.

The timing of the play strategy in relation to the electoral and economic cycle is also telling. In 2007/2008, the Labour Government was a couple of years away from a general election. It is not hard to imagine the political appeal of a significant, visible investment in improving the quality of life of children and young people, at a time when both children's policy and children's well-being were high on the public policy agenda. Lest we forget, this was before the global financial crisis brought almost all new government spending initiatives to a halt.

Whatever the government's motives, this growth in public policy interest in play was also supported by other factors that were under the control (or at least the influence) of play advocates. Over the period under scrutiny, the play sector had taken some key steps to raise its profile, standing and credibility. We showed we were a group that government, charities, public bodies and the private sector could do business with. We fought less amongst ourselves (and did so less publicly). We took seriously the demand for evidence – in particular, for evidence of the difference that good play provision can make. We sought out influential allies such as the high-street children's charity Barnardos, who partnered the Children's Play Council on an early National Lottery funding programme. We learnt how to use the media to get our messages across, most obviously through the Playday campaign and play celebration, which still takes place every August. Perhaps most importantly, we gave a clear narrative about play, why it matters, and why the decline in children's opportunities to play was worthy of government action – linking our story to growing concerns about children's health and well-being.

The US investment bank Lehman Bros filed for bankruptcy just a few months after the play strategy was launched. The subsequent global financial crisis provided the 2010 coalition government with a perfect rationale for scrapping it. Since then, the years of austerity have seen play services decimated and shrinking investment in public play spaces, while Play England and other English play agencies have been fighting for their survival.

This plummeting in the status of play makes it hard to find much evidence of a policy legacy from the Good Times (though the more tangible legacy of thousands of new and improved play areas should not be ignored). Look hard enough, and some crumbs of comfort can be found. Play services in many areas have survived in some form (as in the London Borough of Islington, noted above) where they might otherwise have been axed altogether. So has Play England, thanks largely to a couple of government-funded projects (one linked to volunteering, the other to physical activity). While this clearly marks a move away from support for play for its own sake, arguably the coalition government could have shown even less interest in the subject. The one noteworthy policy win for play came in October 2010, when a government review into health and safety called for action recommended a more balanced approach to risk management in play provision (specifically, the move from risk assessment to risk-benefit assessment). As a result, in 2012 the Health and Safety Executive – the government's safety regulator – issued a statement supporting this move.[8]

As for the future, who knows? In June 2010 Deputy Prime Minister Nick Clegg gave a speech on childhood in which he declared that he wanted to see 'spaces where children can play, where they can feel completely free, where they can safely push at the boundaries, learning and experimenting. Places where different generations can meet, binding the community together'. Writing this in late 2013, I await some concrete actions that might do justice to these fine words. I am not holding my breath.

Acknowledgements

Thanks to Adrian Voce for his help in correcting some factual inaccuracies in a draft of this paper.

Disclosure statement

No potential conflict of interest was reported by the author.

Notes

1. This paper focuses on England. In the late 1990s devolved administrations were created in Wales, Scotland and Northern Ireland. Policy on play and related topics was to a large extent devolved as part of this change, and hence has evolved differently in each of these four parts of the UK.
2. Table 1 sources are as follows:
   1999: author's knowledge.
   2000: Ludvigsen Anna, Creegan Chris, Mills Helen (2005) *Let's Play Together: Play and Inclusion, Evaluation of Better Play Round Three* (Barnardos), 4, Retrieved September 26, 2013, http://www.barnardos.org.uk/lets_play_together_report.pdf.
   2001: Big Lottery Fund website, Retrieved September 26, 2013, http://www.biglotteryfund.org.uk/global-content/programmes/england/childrens-play.
   2007: National Archives website, Retrieved September 26, 2013, http://webarchive.nationalarchives.gov.uk/20090707073355/dcsf.gov.uk/play/. The final figure spent may be nearer £215 million, as an unknown amount was clawed back from local authorities by the Government (Adrian Voce, former Chief Executive of Play England, personal communication).
3. Chris Smith's statement is quoted in Voce, (2008).
4. Paul Hocker (Play Development Team Manager, London Play) personal communication.
5. May 2001 Labour Party press release. As Director of the Children's Play Council at the time, I was passed a copy of a fax of this release by officials from Chris Smith's department. I can find no other primary record of it, though it is referred to in a letter from Adrian Voce to the *Guardian* published on 12 June 2001 (a week or so after the General Election), accessed 7 August 2014: http://www.theguardian.com/theguardian/2001/jun/12/guardianletters. The steps taken by the play sector are discussed in Voce (2008). The £200 million figure is stated in Dobson (2005). £155 million is documented in Hansard (HC Deb, 14 June 2005, c189).
6. These figures come from Chamberlain, George, Golden, Walker, & Benton (2010). The survey does not show why children's ratings rose so much, and the timing of the survey suggests that other factors may have been involved (as is discussed in the report).
7. BBC website, accessed 26 September 2013, http://news.bbc.co.uk/1/hi/education/7156741.stm; UNICEF (2007).

8. The health and safety review is Lord Young of Graffham (2010), *Common Sense, Common Safety*, London: Cabinet Office. The Health and Safety Executive statement is entitled *Children's Play and Leisure: Promoting a Balanced Approach* and is available from the HSE website.

ORCID

Tim Gill ⓘ http://orcid.org/0000-0002-7586-9654

References

Chamberlain, T., George, N., Golden, S., Walker, F., & Benton, T. (2010). *Tellus4 National report* (pp. 51–52). London: Department for Children, Schools and Families.

Dobson, F. (2005) *Getting serious about play* (p. 3). London: Department for Culture, Media and Sport.

UNICEF (2007). *Child poverty in perspective: An overview of child well-being in rich countries, Innocenti Report Card 7* (pp. 2). Florence: UNICEF Innocenti Research Centre.

Voce, A. (2008) 'The State of Play in England'. In F. Brown and C. Taylor (Eds.), *Foundations of playwork* (pp. 23–24). Maidenhead: Open University Press.

HOW WE GOT HERE

The Big Lottery Fund's *Children's Play Programme*: a missed opportunity to gather the evidence?

Alexandra Long

The Big Lottery Fund's Children's Play Programme provided an ideal opportunity to gather evidence of the benefits of funding children's play provision. This paper proposes that without a systematic evaluation of the programme at a national level, an opportunity to evaluate consistently, the impact of the funding on outcomes for children's play was missed.

In 2001, the UK Government pledged that '£200 million of National Lottery money would be earmarked for new and improved children's play facilities' (DCMS, 2004, p. 3). As the most significant investment in children's play provision in terms of scale and distribution at that time (Smith & Day, 2011), the UK Government was determined to ensure the funding was spent to greatest effect. As a result, a national strategy was developed, at the request of the Culture Secretary Tessa Jowell, and 'Getting Serious About Play – A review of children's play' (*GSAP*) was published in 2004 (DCMS, 2004).

GSAP outlined various recommendations on which the Big Lottery Fund's (BLF) Children's Play Initiative was based. Between 2006 and 2012 the BLF *Children's Play Programme* (an element of the Children's Play Initiative) allocated £123 million to 351 Local Authorities in England, to 'create, improve and develop children and young people's free local play spaces and opportunities' (BLF, 2006). This resulted in funding for 1466 individual children's play projects and included a mixture of capital and revenue funding. A diverse range of play projects were funded including: supervised play facilities, investments in play equipment, staffed play ranger projects and the development and improvement of traditional playgrounds (Smith & Day, 2011).

The *Children's Play Programme* and *GSAP* were informed by the document 'Best Play' (NPFA et al., 2000), which identified clear outcomes for children's play provision (Voce, 2008 and Table 1) and was developed in response to a challenge by Government for the play sector to demonstrate the importance of play in children's lives. *Best Play* was relevant to the field of public play provision, and to both supervised and unsupervised play services. The document was 'the first attempt to identify the benefits of play provision in a form that [could] be the basis for evaluation' (NPFA et al., 2000, p. 5).

Table 1.   Best Play 'Objectives for Play Provision'.

Number	Description
1.	The provision extends the choice and control that children have over their play, the freedom they enjoy and the satisfaction they gain from it
2.	The provision recognises the child's need to test boundaries and responds positively to that need
3.	The provision manages the balance between the need to offer risk and the need to keep children safe from harm
4.	The provision maximises the range of play opportunities
5.	The provision fosters independence and self-esteem
6.	The provision fosters children's respect for others and offers opportunities for social interaction
7.	The provision fosters the child's well-being, healthy growth and development, knowledge and understanding, creativity and capacity to learn

Source: NPFA et al. (2006).

The authors of *GSAP* identified that, at the time of publishing, despite the volume of evidence that existed about the benefits of play, almost no work had been undertaken to evaluate the impact of play provision for children. Recognising this, one recommendation for the investment included that:

> ... [the funder] should evaluate the impact on children and young people, parents and local communities of the play projects they fund and also build up a database of what works and what does not. (DCMS, 2004, p. 7)

At a local level, the *BLF* required each Local Authority that was in receipt of funds, to undertake a self-evaluation. The funding guidance stated ' ... you [the local authority] are in charge of the [self-evaluation] process and we would not normally ask to see any report' (BLF, 2006, p. 16). It is widely accepted that making such vague recommendations for evaluation is problematic (Newcomer, Hatry, & Wholey, 2010; Quinn-Patton, 2008; Radhakrishna & Relado, 2009; Taylor, Purdue, Wilson, & Wilde, 2005). Understanding how programme managers view evaluation influences the way in which evaluation is undertaken and the way in which the findings are used, which ultimately impacts on the utility of the evaluation process.

As the DCMS had intimated, the BLF's *Children's Play Programme* provided an ideal opportunity to develop a comprehensive evidence base of the impact of investing in children's play provision. The *Best Play* objectives offered a standardised framework against which each of the 1466 projects could be evaluated (Table 1). However, what transpired for this country-wide programme delivered by 351 different Local Authorities was a distinct lack of a standardised approach to evaluating and monitoring the programme at a project level (Long, 2012). In 2011, the national evaluation of the programme concurred that this was an opportunity missed to evaluate consistently the impact of the funding on outcomes for children, due to a lack of coherence between the monitoring data and outcome measures. Smith and Day argued that:

> ... the common monitoring framework, based on the seven objectives of 'Best Play' ... was not entirely successful in capturing the data that would be required to assess objectively whether the program achieved all of the strategic aims. (2011, p. 8)

The national evaluation tended to focus on programme activities and outputs, which the Department for Children, Schools and Families (DCSF) identify as 'service specifications, delivery mechanisms and procedures' rather than outcomes which DCSF defined as 'end results, they can describe different aspects of well-being for whole populations ... or they can refer to the well-being achieved for users of a particular service or intervention over time' (DCSF, 2008, p. 7).

Furthermore, data for the national evaluation were generated through surveying local authority representatives and individual project managers. It was on this basis that claims for the impact of the programme on children, young people and the local community were based. As such, claims by Smith and Day for 'outcomes' for children, young people and communities are based on a 'subjective assessment of the Programme's success' and carry 'some degree of positive bias' (2011, p. 40). Setting aside issues of bias and subjectivity, the national programme design was systematically weakened in that it allowed adult service providers to speak on behalf of child service users.

There are similarities between this and Lloyd and Harrington's (2012) case study of Sure Start Local Programmes – another UK-based, large-scale, complex national initiative. They too found a mismatch between the local and national evaluation, which resulted in local-level data not being integrated into the national evaluation. The authors identified this as a 'missed opportunity' (p. 97) which resulted in a lack of meaningful evidence of the impact of the Sure Start Programme. This was attributed to the level of autonomy regarding what and when the individual Sure Start projects evaluated, which resulted in difficulties demonstrating the impact of the funding at a national level.

Although because of this disjuncture between the national evaluation and local-level evaluations, it was argued that the national evaluation of the *Children's Play Programme* avoided an 'an overly prescriptive approach to describing and measuring outcomes from play' (Smith & Day, 2011, p. 6), less positively, this implies that the aspirations of *GSAP* to evaluate the impact of the funding on children and young people, parents and local communities were not achieved.

Now that the *Children's Play Programme* has finished, the question of legacy emerges. The investment presented an opportunity to gather evidence, which would support subsequent claims for sustained funding for children's play provision in its various forms in England. Despite 'the various benefits of play [being] beyond doubt' (Hännikainen, Singer, & van Oers, 2013, p. 165), the current UK Government continues to fail to commit to a 'clear policy on children's play' (Play England, 2011a), and play provision in England continues to be hit hard as a result of the austerity measures (Joswiak, 2014; McKendrick et al. in the introduction to this collection; Play England, 2011b). The failure to capitalise upon the opportunity to provide a strong evidence-based case for national play investment is all the more important if, as Newcomer et al. (2010) contend, when credible evaluation findings are communicated to funders, policy and programme management, decisions can be influenced.

The UK Government is placing an increased emphasis on early intervention to address poor outcomes for children (Comptroller and Auditor General, 2013). Early intervention, in this regard, is identified as being about improving the 'essential social and emotional capabilities' of babies, children and young people need for the rest of their lives (Allan, 2011a, p. 1). Allan's independent review of early intervention as a mechanism for 'smarter investment, massive savings'(Allan, 2011a, p. vii) called for early intervention to take a central role in UK policy and practice, and recommended a focusing of investment towards 'early intervention programmes with robust evidence based evaluation systems' (2011b, p. xix). For many years, a wide range of professionals, from within play and beyond, have articulated the value of play in the early development of children (e.g. Shipley, 2012).

However, recent announcements by the Department for Education highlight a distinct lack of understanding of the value of play for the developing child, dismissing the need to allow children opportunities to play freely during their early childhood. Consultations on a review of qualifications for practitioners engaged in care for children under the age of five years, and the regulation and inspection of childcare, reveal a distinct lack of value placed on providing play opportunities for the developing child (Department for Education, 2013). Instead, the developmental benefits of play for young children are being overridden by a move towards formal early education.

Beunderman (2010) suggests that as long as play is accepted as having beneficial effects and is relevant in and of itself, then the key variable is the extent to which children can access it. This view correlates with Russell and Lester's (2008) proposition that play provision should be judged on whether or not it enables children to play, rather than on other instrumental outcomes. However, current developments within UK Government policy suggest that evidencing differential access to play will not, per se, encourage investment to redress such imbalances. Lloyd and Harrington highlight the increased demand for evidence of the impact and outcomes to arise from national initiatives, suggesting that having a solid evidence base of impact and outcomes can help to 'safeguard effective services by providing valuable evidence of the efficacy of initiatives and the need for continued funding' (2012, p. 96). As such, the evidence base of the argument for continued and new funding for children's play needs to be strengthened. The BLF offered an opportunity to capture evaluation evidence on a large scale. This was an opportunity missed. If children's play in England is to be considered an 'effective service', more needs to be done to provide evaluation evidence to support this claim.

Disclosure statement

No potential conflict of interest was reported by the author.

References

Allan, G. (2011a). *Early intervention: Smart investment, massive savings. The second independent report to Her Majesty's Government*. London: HM Government.

Allan, G. (2011b). *Early intervention: Next steps: An independent report to Her Majesty's Government*. London: HM Government.

Beunderman, J. (2010). *People make play: The impact of staffed play provision on children, families and communities. A research report written by DEMOS for Play England*. London: Play England.

BLF. (2006). *England. Children's play programme guidance notes*. London: Author.

Comptroller and Auditor General. (2013). *Early action: Landscape review*. London: National Audit Office.

DCMS. (2004). *Getting serious about play: A review of children's play*. London: TSO.

DCSF. (2008). *Better outcomes for children and young people – from talk to action*. London: TSO.

Department for Education. (2013). "Consultation on early education and childcare staff deployment." *Department for education e-consultations*. London: TSO. Retrieved November 17, 2013, from https://www.education.gov.uk/consultations/index.cfm?action=conResults&consultationId=1866&external=no&menu=3

Hännikainen, M., Singer, E., & van Oers, B. (2013). Promoting play for a better future. *European Early Childhood Education Research Journal, 21*(2), 165–171.

Joswiak, G. (2014). Outdoor play under threat from local facilities and funding cull. *Children and Young People Now*, 7 January 2014.

Lloyd, N., & Harrington, L. (2012). The challenges to effective outcome evaluation of a national, multi-agency initiative: The experience of Sure Start. *Evaluation, 18*(1), 93–109.

Long, A. (2012). *The Big Lottery Fund Children's Play Programme. Getting Serious About Play?* (Masters by Research Thesis). Leeds Metropolitan University.

Newcomer, K., Hatry, H., and Wholey, J. (2010). Planning and designing useful evaluations. In K. Newcomer, H. Hatry, & Wholey, J. Jossey-Bass (Eds.), *Handbook of practical program evaluation* (pp. 5–29, 3rd ed.). San Francisco: Jossey-Bass.

NPFA, Children's Play Council and Playlink. (2000). *Best play: What play provision should do for children.* London: NPFA.

Play England. (2011a). *Children's charity warns that government cuts to play will harm children.* 10 March, 2011. Play England. Retrieved November 17, 2013, from http://www.playengland.org.uk/news/2011/03/chidren's-charity-warns-that-government-cuts-to-play-will-harm-children-.aspx

Play England. (2011b). *Save children's play: Action pack.* Retrieved November 17, 2013, from http://www.playengland.org.uk/resources/save-children's-play-action-pack.aspx

Quinn-Patton, M. (2008). *Utilization-focused evaluation* (4th ed.). London: Sage.

Radhakrishna, R., & Relado, R. (2009). A framework to link evaluation questions to programme outcomes. *Journal of Extension, 47*(3), 7. [online]. Retrieved November 17, 2013, from http://www.joe.org/joe/2009june/pdf/JOE_v47_3tt2.pdf

Russell, W., & Lester, S. (2008). *Play for a change: Play policy and practice. A review of contemporary perspectives.* London: Play England.

Shipley, D. (2012). *Empowering children. Play based curriculum for lifelong learning* (5th ed.). Toronto: Nelson Education.

Smith, N., & Day, L. (2011). *Children's Play Programme Evaluation. Final report to Big Lottery Fund.* November 2011. ECORYS.

Taylor, M., Purdue, D., Wilson, M., & Wilde, P. (2005). *Evaluating community projects – a practical guide.* York: JRF.

Voce, A. (2008). The state of play in England. In F. Brown and C. Taylor (Eds.), *Foundations of playwork* (pp. 22–25). Maidenhead: Open University Press.

AUSTERITY AS THREAT

Slip sliding away: a case study of the impact of public sector cuts on some of the services supporting children's play opportunities in the city of Sheffield in the north of England

Helen Woolley

Since the UK general election of 2010 the government has entered into a programme of financial cuts affecting local authority services dramatically. This is especially the situation for sectors such as play (and green spaces) which are not statutory. Sheffield is a city in the north of England and this paper gives an insight into some of the impact that these massive financial cuts have had on local provision, either directly by local government or through voluntary and other organisations. Two adventure playgrounds in the city provide examples of the effect of the austerity measures and how the local communities are now involved in managing these important facilities.

Introduction and methodology

This paper explores the impact on some of the provision for play, and to a lesser extent sport, of financial expenditure cuts in the city of Sheffield in northern England. This paper is exploratory, undertaken in the early stages of the process to begin to understand something of the situation. The research that underpins the paper was undertaken in a purposive manner for the *Play in Times of Austerity* seminar (see McKendrick et al., in the introduction to this collection) over a short period of time during April and May 2013. The methodology comprised three elements: an analysis of publically available documents sourced through an online search, three interviews with key informants with some interest or responsibility for the provision of play in Sheffield, and an informal discussion with a group of volunteers involved with an adventure playground in the north of the city.

The interviewees were: a member of staff from Activity Sheffield who discussed information which was publically available; the Manager, together with input from staff members of a long-established charity supporting pre-school learning; and an individual who for 10 years managed a Sure Start centre in one of the most deprived areas of the city. An ethics review was undertaken and approved by the author's departmental Research Ethics Committee.

The information gathered provides insight at one particular point in time as to how public spending cuts are affecting key aspects of the service provision pertaining to children's play, and to a lesser extent sport, in Sheffield. Two cautions should be acknowledged: first, there are many others involved in these matters across the city who were not interviewed; and second, in the time between undertaking the interviews and writing this paper and its publication public sector funding cuts have continued and the context of funding and facilities will have changed, presumably to intensify the dis-benefit to children and play opportunities.

Strategic-level support

The City of Sheffield is the fourth largest city in England and has a population of 551,800 (Sheffield City Council, n.d., a). *Activity Sheffield* provides 'play, dance, sport and healthy activities for all ages across the city' (Sheffield City Council, n.d., b). From the financial year 2011/2012, the budget for *Activity Sheffield* was £2.1 million and this reduced to £1.4 million in 2012/13 and £1.0 million in 2013/14: a reduction of over 50% in 3 years.

Funding external to the local authority had been available from sources such as national government and the BIG Lottery for projects including the Homeless Play Project (Sheffield City Council, 2013), and the BIG Lottery, the Play Builder programme (which supported the redesign and build of outdoor play spaces), and *Kids Can Do* (a programme of activities including play workers to support children's activities between 2008 and 2013 – Sheffield City Council, n.d., c). A Play Partnership, bringing together a range of individuals and organisations interested in play across the city existed from 2007 to 2010. Similar organisations were established in many English cities, because they were an integral part of the national drive at that time to support play (Play England, 2011). Following the 'austerity cuts' that were introduced by the new UK Government after the general election of 2010, the Play Partnership in Sheffield combined with other city organisations to become *Go Sheffield*, where the main interest and driver is sport and not play. *Activity Sheffield* used to support various sports including athletics, football and swimming; the former are no longer supported and the latter is now being supported for one final year. Cuts to play services are equally severe. Rangers worked across the play and parks sectors providing play-related activities, such as events in parks, holiday clubs, bug hunts, pond dipping and two sessions a year in each primary school. The budget for Rangers was reduced from £700,000 to £350,000 and their role was reduced to only undertaking woodland maintenance. In addition, organisations such as the *Out of School Network*; the *Sheffield Information Link* and the *Sheffield City Childcare Network* all disappeared in 2012.

A sector in decline I: reduction of Sure Start early years provision

The funding for the early years sector has reduced over the past years and the city council was expecting a further £6.8 million reduction in the Early Intervention Grant (EIG), received from national Government, in the 2013/14 allocations. Additionally, in future years, the EIG will be incorporated into the Revenue Support Grant (RSG), rather than being separately identifiable. The RSG is also facing further budget reductions in 2014/15. The inclusion of the EIG into the RSG will result in specific funding for early years being lost and the possibility that the transparency of early years funding will become obscured, and the pressures on funding that was ring fenced for early years may be increased, in the future.

The Sure Start programme was initiated by the Labour government and in Sheffield 36 Sure Start Centres were established. As a result of the public sector funding cuts these were reorganised into 17 Children's Centres, each covering a larger geographic area, in 2013. In addition, grants to 16 childcare providers in the Private, Voluntary and Independent sector and to four providers in the statutory sector have ceased. In the early days of the Sure Start programme, there was a direct relationship with the Government Regional Office. In 2005/6 the funding and relationship was devolved from the Government Regional Office to Local Authorities. At first, the funding was ring fenced. However, as the money available has reduced (the £10 million budget for the Sure Start service in Sheffield was reduced to £4million by 2011), the ring-fencing was removed. Thus early years funding has supported play through Sure Start Centres and provision for such play opportunities has contracted as Sure Start centres have closed.

A strong feeling was expressed by one interviewee that partly as a result of the early years sector sitting within the City of Sheffield's Directorate of Children's Services alongside Education, and partly as a consequence of Sheffield being a large city, the early years sector had low political priority locally, and much less than the interviewee and other workers would have liked. One Sure Start centre, first established in 2002, now operates with a single desk and telephone. This centre serves 1600 children in deprivation. It previously employed 36 staff (18 full-time equivalent) with the capacity to engage families speaking 16 different languages. The budget of this centre has reduced from £800,000 in 2002 to £260,000 in 2011 and at the time of interview had a staff level of 3.5 full-time equivalent. Subsequently this was closed in September 2013.

A sector in decline II: The death of a long-established charity?

A national charity which works to support the early years sector was established nationally more than 50 years ago and 47 years ago in Sheffield. During the last 5–10 years, as the range of external funding sources has declined, the Sheffield office has increasingly supported work in the neighbouring towns of Rotherham, Barnsley and Doncaster. In 2010/11 the Sheffield office's income was £400,000. This reduced to £360,00 in 2011/12; £330,000 in 2012/13, and £0 in 2013/14. The local organisation is surviving for 6 months on funding from the assets of the national organisation, while it seeks to establish other funding.

These financial reductions mean that the organisation is no longer able to support development work in 25 settings each year to assist with the appraisal of the quality of indoor and outdoor play areas for OFSTED inspections. There has also been a cut in safeguarding training and an abolition of the Special Needs Project which was supporting 45 children and families when the funding was withdrawn on 31 March 2013, and which had supported about 1800 individual children with special needs, and their families over a 13-year period.

Overall, the concerns of this charity are that both the safety and the quality of early years settings in Sheffield and across the wider South Yorkshire Region will be compromised. Currently, early years settings with a 'good' OFSTED report obtain Government funding and the charity is concerned that without support some of these settings will not be able to retain their 'good' rating and will therefore lose their funding. The charity has already received feedback from staff in the settings it supports. The staff have articulated concerns about: losing on-going support; a lack of awareness about new initiatives; having no-where to go to for help when they experience a crisis; and not being able to draw on assistance for future staff recruitment.

On the positive side, the charity considered that it was now operating in a more business-like manner, improving the way in which it communicated internally, and was being more innovative than hitherto. However, not all changes were necessarily welcomed; it realised that it would have to change its philosophy and that future work may not always be engaging disadvantaged communities.

Individual provision: What future for adventure playgrounds?

Sheffield has two adventure playgrounds, both in relatively deprived areas with multi-cultural communities; one to the north and the other to the south of the city centre (Sheffield City Council, n.d., d). A sum of £176,000 used to be allocated annually for both adventure playgrounds, which faciliated the opening of each centre for five hours a day, five days a week. As part of the 'austerity cuts', closure was proposed for both adventure playgrounds at the end of March 2013. However, both playgrounds had considerable community support and campaigns were organised to contest the proposals (e.g. Sheffield City Council, n.d., e).

Sheffield City Council agreed to transition arrangements for each facility being open for three hours a day, three days a week for two months until the end of May 2013. The member of staff from the city council suggested that the two adventure playgrounds were quite different in terms of their physical and social context. The site to the north of the city centre (Pitsmoor Adventure Playground) was characterised by the City Council thus:

- it has more traditional self-build features. It is therefore 'higher risk' and Sheffield City Council do not consider that it can become an 'open' playground;
- it is not located on a bus route and not easily seen;
- it is next door to a rehabilitation centre, which means that when the adventure playground was staffed any issues arising from this could be dealt with;
- there is not a group of people who are ready and able to continue the on-going management of the site and
- the first public meeting was attended by 30–50 people, but only six or seven people showed an interest in saving the site a few months hence.

In contrast, the Council Officer summarised the context of the site to the south of the city (Highfields Adventure Playgrounds) thus:

- it contains less self-build elements than the other adventure playground, meaning it would be easier to convert to an 'open playground';
- it is open for younger age groups;
- some parents use it as a childcare facility;
- it has the support of the local community forum;
- it is located on a bus route and
- it has a group of committed people who support its continued existence; one of whom is a teacher of vulnerable children at a secondary school, but who works with children in the playground.

In light of these differences, the Council Officer felt that it was more likely that the Highfield Adventure Playground would succeed: partly because it had the possibility to become an open access playground, but also because it had a group of people whom it was considered could take the future management of the site forward.

A small group of individuals at the Pitsmoor Adventure Playground to the north of the city centre, which was established by parents in the mid-1970s, felt aggrieved at the way that the City Council had made the decision to reduce the hours and threaten its closure. Their understanding was that the financial calculations that the City Council had undertaken comparing the financial support to sports vans visiting parks, which Activity Sheffield provided at times such as school holidays, and to adventure playgrounds had not been undertaken equitably. They also felt very strongly that the social and community benefit of the adventure playground was not being taken into account. The site was used by forty, sometimes up to 100, children most days after school and just 2 weeks earlier an event had been held that had attracted 250 people. The police go to the adventure playground and play football and organise mountain bike sessions with the children building up positive relationships. The perception that the council was underestimating the social importance of the site was also partly driven by an understanding and knowledge that when children are not at the adventure playground, some of them are mixing with adults who are drug dealing and that there had been a local drug-related gun murder in recent years. Concern was also expressed that the users of the playground would not be in a position to go to the lengths of constituting a voluntary organisation to take the site forward. It was considered that any such organisation would need enabling support (a point also acknowledged by the Council Officer) and therefore was different from the other adventure playground in the city.

Subsequent to these interviews, Pitsmoor Adventure Playground was indeed closed until further notice (Sheffield City Council, n.d., d). At the time of writing, Highfields Adventure Playground remained open as an adventure playground , but with reduced hours of three hours per day, for three days a week (Sheffield City Council, n.d., d). Back in April and prior to the closure of Pitsmoor, evidence was emerging of its pending decline; 2 days before I visited this adventure playground the slide had been removed by the City Council with the explanation that it was 'unsafe'. Apparently no risk benefit analysis had been undertaken for the slide. The slide had slipped away.

Conclusion: move from City Council to local community management

Across the City of Sheffield, services and support for children's play are being dramatically reduced. Negative impacts will result from the decrease in budget to *Activity Sheffield*; changes within the Council's budget that will result in early years funding not being ring-fenced; reorganisation of Sure Start centres; cuts in funding to charities and community organisations; loss of adventure playgrounds; loss of staff to support play (and sport or environmental activities); together with issues such as financial cuts to the parks and countryside service; and changes in local governance. Cuts will no doubt continue to be introduced and services will no doubt continue to contract at different levels: strategic and city; sector; and individual site and delivery. The Council Officer who was interviewed reflected on the situation expressing that they felt like saying to people: 'you have some support now ... you can't rely on us forever ... we aren't going to be here'.

This can all be understood within the context of the fact that for many years Sheffield marketed itself as *The National City of Sport*, being designated as such by the Sports Council in 1995 (Local Government Chronicle, 1995). Yet, it has now closed, and in late 2013 demolished the award-winning Don Valley Athletics Stadium. If it is forgoing one of its most prestigious sports facilities what does this mean in the longer term for all public facilities, parks and people supporting children's play – are they set to 'slip slide away' like the slide at the Pitsmoor Adventure Playground?

Two-and-a-half years since the original research all Local Authority funding has been withdrawn from the adventure playgrounds and the charity supporting early years provision. The 16 Sure Start centres exist with a much reduced service with some now being in libraries and primary schools and the previously used buildings being vacant. From the City Council web site, it appears that much of what is now offered is a range of clinics and information about other activities (https://www.sheffield.gov.uk/education/information-for-parentscarers/care-support/childcare/childrens-centres/valley-park.html [Accessed 2 September 2015]).

Pitsmoor Adventure Playground is being managed by a charitable organisation established by local people, has qualified staff and is open for three hours a day, four days a week both in term time and school holidays. (https://pitsmooradventureplayground.wordpress.com/ [Accessed 2 August 2015]).

Highfield Adventure Playground is managed by the Sharrow Community Forum with a community group, Friends of Adventures, supporting the playground. It is staffed and open for three hours a week on 3 days in term times and as advertised in school holidays. They are also about to re-introduce loose parts on the site. (http://sharrowcf.org.uk/highfield-adventure-playground-2/ [Accessed 2 August 2015]).

So the savage cuts to public sector funding has closed some of the provision where children were supported in their play. However there are three notable changes for these longstanding facilities. First both adventure playgrounds are now being run by local community groups not the Local Authority. Second there is a re-introduction of loose parts. Third there is a focus on a risk benefit approach rather than the risk assessment approach previously adhered to by the City Council. These three changes alone indicates that the adventure playgrounds are becoming more characteristic of the original adventure playground movement which is perhaps an unexpected benefit of the withdrawal of local authority funding.

Disclosure statement

No potential conflict of interest was reported by the author.

References

Local Government Chronicle. (1995). Sheffield to be first official national city of sport. *Local Government Chronicle.* 14 July, 1995. Retrieved November 17, 2013, from http://www.lgcplus.com/sheffield-to-be-first-official-national-city-of-sport/1574480.article

Play England. (2011). Creating successful play partnerships. *Community Play Briefing 2.* Play England. Retrieved November 17, 2013, from http://www.playengland.org.uk/media/281629/playpartnerships_briefing_ver5%20-%20final.pdf

Sheffield City Council. (2013). *Places for people: Windmill Lane Project.* Updated October 2, 2013. Retrieved November 17, 2013, from http://www.sheffieldhelpyourself.org.uk/full_search_new.asp?group=24691

Sheffield City Council. (n.d., a). *Sheffield facts and figures.* Retrieved November 17, 2013, from https://www.sheffield.gov.uk/your-city-council/sheffield-profile.html

Sheffield City Council. (n.d., b). *Activities (activity Sheffield).* Retrieved November 17, 2013, from https://www.sheffield.gov.uk/out–about/leisure/activities.html

Sheffield City Council. (n.d., c). *Kids can do positive activities (8–13).* Retrieved November 17, 2013, from https://www.sheffield.gov.uk/education/about-us/projects-initiatives/kidscando

Sheffield City Council. (n.d., d). *Adventure playgrounds.* Retrieved November 17, 2013, from https://www.sheffield.gov.uk/out–about/leisure/leisure-facilities/adventure-playgrounds.html

Sheffield City Council. (n.d., e). *Save Highfield Adventure Playground.* E-Petitions. Retrieved November 17, 2013, from https://sheffield.moderngov.co.uk/mgEPetitionDisplay.aspx?id=96

AUSTERITY AS A THREAT

Playwork practitioners' perceptions of the impact on play of austerity in the UK: comparing experiences in Scotland and SW England

John H. McKendrick and Chris Martin

This paper compares playworkers' perception of the extent to which Austerity has changed playworkers' working environment, children's opportunities to play and the context within which play takes place in Scotland and SW England, regions which are understood to have divergent experiences in recent years. 351 playworkers completed a bespoke survey, comprising 33 questions, for which a variety of distributions modes were used and the result of which was a survey population that was broadly representative of respondents to the last major national survey of playworkers in Great Britain. Two themes emerge. First, in many ways, the experience of play in 2013 differed between playwork practitioners in Scotland and SW England. Statistically significant differences were found for most of the organisational issues, half of the regional issues, and both of the indicators of overall satisfaction. In each instance where a difference was observed, conditions in 2013 had worsened more in SW England than in Scotland. Thus, it is problematic to portray a 'global' experience of play in the UK and the existing ancedotal and case study evidence contrasting the fortunes of play in England and Scotland in 2013 are acknowledged by, and find expression through, playwork practitioners' reflections on their work. Second, and on the other hand, in SW England, the more strongly negative experience of government (both national and local) in relation to play in 2013 and the negative perception of wider play and playwork trends in the SW region contrast sharply with positive experiences of play and playwork in the workplace. It is also argued that the divergent understandings of play in SW England are suggestive of the merit of research that pursue holistic appraisals of playwork.

Play and austerity

Few would dispute the assertion that austerity in the UK has impacted on services for children's play. The logic of the shift being engineered by the UK government away from 'big government' towards 'big society and the leaner state' (Kane & Allen, 2011; McKendrick et al., 2015) and the array of ancedotal and qualitative case study evidence on the loss of funding, facilities, services and staff for play in individual local authorities (Gove, 2010; Hayes, 2014; Joswiak, 2012; Martin, 2014; Morton, 2012; Play England, 2011; Play in Peril, 2013; UNITE, 2013; Vasagar, 2010; Woolley, 2015) would also tend to suggest that public provision of play opportunities is being curtailed. However, the situation is complex and it would be premature to conclude that these changes to public provision are solely having an adverse impact on childhood play, which is something children do with or without an adult presence. Furthermore, the logic of the change envisaged by the UK government is that the Third sector (in its various guises) and the private sector develop to replace the gap left behind by the withdrawal of government-led strategic planning and funding, and local authority financial support and service provision. The recent growth of the 'street play' movement in the UK (Hocker, 2014; Ferguson and Page, 2015) may be indicative of a shift in the balance of adult-supported play away from the playwork model, which may, in turn, also alter the profile of children whose play is being supported by direct adult engagement.

It would be instructive to ascertain the extent to which, and the ways in which, these changes are evident across the UK to: appraise whether there has been any net reduction in play capacity (both in terms of play settings and skilled professionals who facilitate play); and examine whether these environmental and personnel changes have impacted upon the quantity and quality of children's play. These questions might best be answered by a nationwide study that canvassed information directly from play service providers and children, respectively. However, playwork practitioners are also well placed to offer informed comment on these issues. Furthermore, there is a need to consider how these changes to play provision are being experienced by the practitioners whose livelihoods depend on them. A survey of playwork practitioners would appear to provide the means to better understand the extent to which austerity has changed their working environment, opportunities for children to play and the context within which play takes place in the UK. Furthermore, it would be interesting to compare and contrast experiences in regions which are understood to have had differing fortunes of play in 2013. These are the themes that are explored in this paper and this is the approach taken. However, this presupposes the possibility, and assumes the utility, of a frame of reference for play that extends beyond the individual region.

National play intelligence in the UK

There is no better example of the utility of a UK national frame of reference for play than *Playday*, the national celebration of children's play in the UK and annual opportunity to promote its value (Playday, n.d.). *Playday* is organised and coordinated jointly by the four sub UK-national play organisations in the UK (Play England, Play Wales, Play Scotland and Playboard Northern Ireland) and is invariably underpinned by a nationwide survey (opinion poll) to provide UK-wide evidence to support the claims for play being advanced in that particular year (Playday, 2010).

A shared sense of purpose in advocating for play in the UK is also promoted through the *Children's Play Policy Forum* (n.d.), which brings together the four sub-UK national play organisations, UK Government departments, 'Home Nation' Government departments and the lead body for play in the Republic of Ireland to 'improve the understanding of, and commitment to, the importance of high quality play opportunities for all children and young people of the United Kingdom and Republic of Ireland'. Briefings and research reports published by one sub-national play organisation are routinely disseminated to the others; further evidence of common purpose and interests.

However, as is discussed by McKendrick et al. in the introduction to this collection, play is the responsibility of the devolved sub-national governments in the UK. The logic of devolution is that local solutions emerge to attend to local needs and, as with many other responsibilities of devolved government in the UK (Leith & McPhee, 2012), policy divergence for play has emerged (McKendrick et al., Introduction to this collection). The shared sense of UK purpose in promoting play is threatened, to some extent, by the four sub-national play organisations needing to focus on defining their own sub-nation's priorities and capitalising on opportunities to promote play that are afforded through devolution. The potential for devolution to fracture a common play landscape in the UK was realised with the significant additional sums of money that were invested in play in England under the devolved funding regimes of the National Lottery in the UK (discussed by Tim Gill in this collection).

However, although play priorities and trajectories have diverged across the UK, this does not necessarily undermine the value of a UK-national frame of reference to understand and appraise play and playwork; indeed, this may be of heightened importance as a result of divergent pathways for play. In the same manner in which the Open Method of Coordination is used to encourage nations in Europe to adopt more progressive strategies to tackle child poverty by highlighting best practice and making transparent differences in the reality of child poverty and policies which are used to tackle it (Heidenreich & Zeitlin, 2009), there may be merit in highlighting divergence in play and playwork across the UK (to strengthen the case in regions where it is less well resourced or supported).

More problematic than divergence might be the difficulties faced in designing and executing UK-wide research on children's play. Although it is straightforward to canvass UK public opinion (and to a lesser extent the opinion of parents and/or children) on matters pertaining to play, it is far less straightforward to specifically canvass opinion of playwork practitioners in the UK. Most importantly, there is no single source of contact for playwork practitioners or playwork employers in the UK. Even the membership registers of the four sub-national organisations for play in the UK do not, in aggregate, provide a comprehensive register of playworkers or play practitioners. Differing levels of attachment to the profession among those delivering what might be considered to be playwork, significant numbers of part-time, casual, volunteer and seasonal staff (SkillsActive, 2010) and the absence of a formal register to which adults working in the children's play sector must belong, all help explain why the regional and sub-national membership lists of playwork bodies are unable to provide a comprehensive register of playworkers or play practitioners.

Faced with these difficulties, Skillsactive in England executed four rounds of *Playwork People*, a biennial survey of the playwork workforce in England from 2003 to 2009 (Skillsactive, 2004, 2006, 2008, 2010). As the largest dedicated survey of playwork in England, it aimed to provide an invaluable source of quantitative information about the characteristics of the workforce through two separate questionnaires: one for both playwork employers and employees, and an additional questionnaire for employers. More specifically, the surveys aimed to: profile the characteristics of the workforce; profile skills and qualification levels; and identify future training requirements. Without a sampling frame for playworkers from which to draw a representative sample, *Playwork People* utilised contact databases, playwork events and snowballing to reach 'as many playworkers as possible'. Self-completion surveys were thus distributed by post, in person at events, via the Internet and by email. The survey population of the last three surveys were 456, 1295 and 575, respectively, for the survey of individuals. Notwithstanding problems induced by selective exposure to the survey, self-selection (only those who perceive themselves to be playworkers or play practitioners were likely to respond) and the general limitations that are encountered through survey research (e.g. higher response rates among the more literate), if used carefully, the *Playwork People* series can be used to comment on the reliability of the survey population in subsequent studies of playworkers in the UK.

Research design

This research aimed to understand playwork practitioners' experience of play and playwork in 2013. More specifically, it sought to ascertain whether the differing fortunes of the play sectors across the UK impacted on playwork practitioners' experiences and perception of their work.

To address these issues, the experiences of playwork practitioners were canvassed in two regions with contrasting experiences in 2013, that is, SW England (which, in common with all English regions, was readjusting to a policy context in which the national (UK) government was less supportive of play – Gove, 2013) and Scotland (which, in contrast, had experienced a year in which the sub-national (Scottish) government had made its first ever commitment to children's play – Scottish Government, 2013). Both regions have comparable populations (5.3 million in both SW England and Scotland, according to the 2011 Census of Population); comprise a mix of cities, large towns and rural areas; and are served by an area-wide organisation that promotes children's play (South West Play Forum and Play Scotland). Furthermore, each author is represented on the body that serves play in their area (Martin on the SW Play Forum and McKendrick on Play Scotland).

A self-completion survey was designed to address the research questions. Profile questions were adapted to facilitate comparison with the survey population in the *Playwork People* surveys. A temporal focus was adopted for the substantive issues, that is, respondents were asked to appraise whether matters had improved, worsened or remained the same (as opposed to determining whether matters were good, neutral or bad). This temporal focus was appropriate for this research which specifically aimed to appraise changes in play in 2013. A 33 question survey was designed, which comprised questions on play and playwork in the region; their playwork in 2013; play in their organisation in 2013; perceptions for play in 2014; and profile questions. This paper is specifically concerned with the experience of play in 2013.

Fieldwork was undertaken towards the end of 2013, with a closing date for return of surveys in mid-December. As with *Playwork People*, a range of strategies were used to distribute surveys with the aim of increasing reach. First and foremost, the SW Play Forum and Play Scotland raised awareness of the research among members, providing weblinks to an online version of the survey. This was supplemented in each region by the authors' directly canvassing private sector providers, Third Sector organisations and local authority contacts for play organisations (SW England – many of which were accessed through their listing in the online directory, netmums. org.uk), and sub-regional play forums (Scotland). These supplementary strategies to reach playwork practitioners were particularly important in SW England, where the response rate to the survey was lower than in Scotland.

By the end of the fieldwork, 351 responses had been received, 284 from Scotland and 67 from SW England. Although the number of responses from SW England, in particular, necessitates cautious interpretation of data, the level of response was deemed adequate to address the research aims. Most importantly, there was more similarity than difference among the survey populations (and between the SW England survey population in 2013 and the *Playwork People* survey population for England in 2009) (Table 1).

Notwithstanding that the survey populations are broadly similar, there are specific compositional differences that are of note. For example, although the profile of respondents from Scotland and SW England are similar in terms of age profile, union membership, length of time as a playworker, and sector in which they work, the survey population in SW England comprises fewer women (although women are still in the majority), more part-time workers, more with a playwork qualification (although the majority in Scotland also have such a qualification), more who define their occupation in terms of a play-defined role, and more serving older children. Similarly, compared to the *Playwork People* surveys, the SW England survey population comprises more younger playwork practitioners, more with longer service as a playworker, and more with playwork qualifications.

However, the decision was taken not to weight the survey populations for analysis given that it cannot be asserted that the *Playwork People* survey populations are representative of playwork

Table 1.   Profile of survey respondents (%).

Gender	Scot	SW	PP4	Duration as playworker	Scot	SW	PP4
% Women	89	66	86	Less than year	5	8	12
Age				1–2 years	6	8	18
Under 24	3	10	7	–5 years	14	18	32
25–34	17	10	37	6–10 years	18	14	17
35–49 (35–44)	49	42	26	More than 10 years	56	51	21
50–59 (45–54)	27	25	28	Occupation (selected)			
Over 59 (Over 54)	4	12	3	Manager	38	30	30
Union Membership				Play-defined	45	70	67
% Yes	14	16	17	Sector (selected)			
Playwork Qualification				Local authority	26	25	25
% With	54	72	56	Private	11	14	32
Age Children Served				No. of Hours Worked			
Pre-school	–	–	78	Less than 30	44	63	72
Early primary	61	78	83	More than 30	47	30	18
Late primary	57	87	88	Irregular	10	8	na
Early secondary	31	74	Na				
Late secondary	16	43	28				

practitioners or playworkers in the UK; differences between the survey populations in 2013 and the last *Playwork People* survey in 2009 may reflect changes to the playwork workforce, rather than sample bias; and differences between the Scottish and SW England survey populations may reflect the different nature of playwork in these regions. It was considered more prudent to adopt an analytical approach in which comparisons of playwork practitioners in SW England and Scotland in 2013 were subjected to three-way analysis to ascertain whether compositional effects account for any differences that emerge. For example, it was considered whether a higher proportion of men in the SW England survey population may account for variation in playwork practitioners' experiences in 2013 between SW England and Scotland. It transpired, however, that compositional factors do not explain differing experiences across these two regions. Indeed, if anything some compositional differences in the survey populations tended to reduce the extent of the variation that was apparent between SW England and Scotland. For example, despite the findings that respondents in Scotland tended to report more favourably on play in 2013 and that those with higher levels of training also had a tendency to report more favourably on play in 2013 (such that it might be expected that more respondents in Scotland had a higher level of training), it transpires that higher levels of training were more characteristic of SW England than Scotland (thereby serving to ameliorate differences in satisfaction with play in 2013 between the two regions). This, together with other similar examples, leads to the conclusion that contextual factors are evident that account for differences in the experience of play in Scotland and SW England in 2013.

The big picture

Respondents were asked to assess their overall satisfaction with play in their area (either Scotland or SW England) using a five point scale ranging from 'strongly increased in 2013' through to 'strongly decreased in 2013' (Figure 1). Opt out options were provided, that is, 'do not know' or 'rather not say'. More detail on the nature of play in their area in 2013 was then canvassed through an eleven-part question in which respondents were asked to appraise whether conditions in 2013 had 'got better', 'stayed the same' or 'got worse'. (Figure 2). Detail was canvassed on five

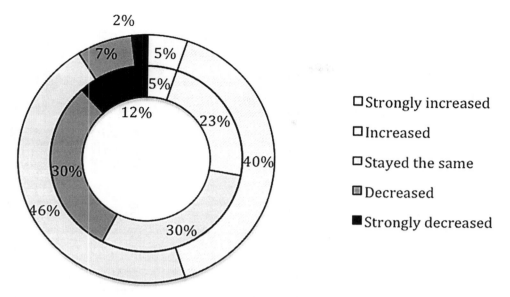

Figure 1.   Satisfaction with play in 2013 in Scotland (outer ring) and SW England (inner ring). Note: Statistically significant difference at the 95% confidence level: Pearson Chi-Square = 44.784, with four degrees of freedom and two cells (20%) with an Expected Frequency of less than five.
Source: Authors' surveys: Scotland ($n = 262$) and SW England ($n = 61$)

themes (government and play; communities and play; parents and play; playspace; and playwork); once again, opt out options were provided.

Satisfaction with play

Although the full gamut of opinion is reported in both Scotland and SW England, there is significantly less dissatisfaction with play in 2013 in Scotland; indeed more than four times as many playwork practitioners in SW England than Scotland expressed decreasing satisfaction with play in 2013 (42%, compared with 9% in Scotland). The vast majority in Scotland reported that their satisfaction had either remained constant in 2013, or had improved (slightly); in SW England, more reported that satisfaction had decreased than increased (45%, compared to 28%).

Government and play

The most striking differences of opinion between playwork practitioners in Scotland and SW England are expressed with regard to the role of government in play in 2013 (Figure 2). Almost twice as many in SW England than Scotland perceive that the amount of money spent by local authorities on children's play had worsened in 2013 (81%, compared to 45%). These findings are not surprising given that overall spending on play by local authorities in England dropped from £67.9 m in 2010/2011 to £26.4 m in 2013/2014 (Joswiak, 2014). Seven times as many in SW England perceived that the national government's commitment to play in 2013 worsened compared to Scotland (82%, compared to 13%).

Levels of dissatisfaction with government (local and national) are clearly evident in SW England. However, the higher levels of dissatisfaction expressed in SW England should not obfuscate the finding that playwork practitioners in Scotland are thrice as likely to consider that local government spending worsened, rather than improved, in 2013 (45%, compared to 15%).

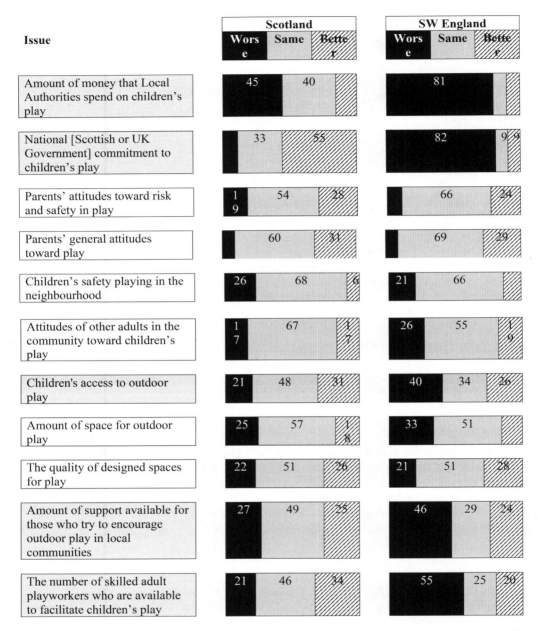

Issue	Scotland			SW England		
	Worse	Same	Better	Worse	Same	Better
Amount of money that Local Authorities spend on children's play	45	40		81		
National [Scottish or UK Government] commitment to children's play	33	55		82	9	9
Parents' attitudes toward risk and safety in play	19	54	28		66	24
Parents' general attitudes toward play		60	31		69	29
Children's safety playing in the neighbourhood	26	68	6	21	66	
Attitudes of other adults in the community toward children's play	17	67	17	26	55	19
Children's access to outdoor play	21	48	31	40	34	26
Amount of space for outdoor play	25	57	18	33	51	
The quality of designed spaces for play	22	51	26	21	51	28
Amount of support available for those who try to encourage outdoor play in local communities	27	49	25	46	29	24
The number of skilled adult playworkers who are available to facilitate children's play	21	46	34	55	25	20

Figure 2. Playwork practitioners' evaluation of changes to play in 2013 for Scotland and SW England (*% of respondents*). Note: Variable labels in shaded cells denote a statistically significant difference in the results between Scotland and SW England at the 95% confidence level.
Source: Authors' surveys: Scotland (*n* = 223–269) and SW England (*n* = 40–50)

Parents and play

In sharp contrast to the findings for 'government and play', perceptions of parental outlook on play are similar among playwork practitioners in Scotland and SW England, with the majority opinion in each case being that attitudes had remained constant in 2013. Among those playwork professionals who discern a change, more were likely to report evidence of 'improvement'. Using 'parents' general attitudes towards children's play' as an example, 31% in Scotland considered that attitudes had improved, compared to 10% who thought that they has worsened; similarly, 29% in SW England considered that parents' attitudes had improved, compared to only 2% who thought that attitudes had worsened.

Communities and play

As for 'parents and play', the dominant perception among playwork practitioners were similar in Scotland and SW England, that is, there had been little change with regards to 'play and communities' in 2013, for example, two thirds of playwork practitioners report that there has been no change with regards to children's safety in their neighbourhood (66% in SW England and 68% in Scotland). Notwithstanding this, almost four times as many playwork practitioners in Scotland, and twice as many in SW England, consider that children's safety playing in the neighbourhood has worsened (rather than improved) in 2013 (26%, compared to 6% for Scotland, and 21%, compared to 13% for SW England).

The broadest spread of opinion in both Scotland and SW England was reported for the issue of 'children's access to outdoor play'. This is also an issue for which there is more difference of opinion across SW England and Scotland. Playwork practitioners in SW England were twice as likely as those in Scotland to consider that children's access to outdoor play had worsened in 2013 (40% in SW England, compared to 21% in Scotland). In Scotland, the modal opinion was that there had been no change in 2013 (with more reporting an improvement than worsening conditions among the remainder), whereas in SW England the most common opinion was that access had worsened.

Playspace

Interestingly, there were no differences expressed by playwork practitioners in Scotland and SW England in terms of whether the quantity or quality of available play spaces had changed in 2013. In each case, the majority considered that there had been no change in 2013, although slightly more perceived that the amount of space for outdoor play had worsened than improved (e.g. 33%, compared to 16% in SW England) and slightly more perceived that the quality of designed spaces for play had improved, rather than worsened (e.g. 26%, compared to 22% in Scotland).

Playwork

Significant differences between playwork practitioners in Scotland and SW England were evident with regard to playwork in 2013. In SW England, the most common opinion was that the number of skilled playworkers who were available to facilitate children's play and the amount of support that was available to encourage outdoor play in local communities has worsened (55% and 46%, respectively), supported from a national perspective by Joswiak (2014); in contrast, in Scotland, the most common opinion was that matters had not changed in 2013 (46% and 49%, respectively). Indeed, more playwork practitioners in Scotland opined that matters had improved than worsened with respect to the number of skilled playworkers (34%, compared to 21%).

Workplace

Respondents were asked a similar set of questions about play in their own organisation (workplace), as they were for play in their region. First, they were asked to assess their overall satisfaction with play in their organisation in 2013 using the same five point scale, with opt out options (Figure 3). More detail on play in their organisation was then canvassed through an eight-part question using the same three point scale as before, with opt out options (Figure 4). Detail on play in their own organisation was canvassed on two themes (play services and playwork).

Satisfaction with play services provided

Playwork practitioners express more satisfaction than dissatisfaction in 2013 with the play services provided by their organisation. For example, 59% in Scotland reported that their satisfaction had increased, compared to 6% who reported that it had decreased or significantly decreased (in SW England, the respective proportions were 48% and 26%, respectively – still numerically positive, but over one quarter of respondents expressing dissatisfaction with their own organisation's play services is significant).

Notably, more satisfaction was expressed with play in their organisation (Figure 3) than with the fortunes of play in their region (Figure 1), that is, 59% in Scotland and 48% in SW England reported that their satisfaction with the services provided by their organisation had increased (Figure 3); this compares to 45% and 28%, respectively, for increasing satisfaction in 2013 for their region (Figure 1).

Services provided

On the whole, playwork practitioners delivered a positive appraisal of the service provided by their organisation in 2013: the majority in both SW England and Scotland opined that the number of children that they reached had improved in 2013 (62% and 58%, respectively); the most common opinion was that the range of play services they provided in 2013 had improved

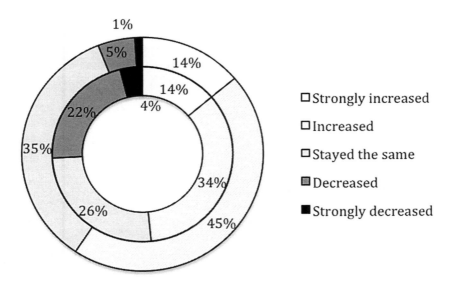

Figure 3.   Satisfaction with play services provided in their own organisation in 2013 in Scotland (outer ring) and SW England (inner ring). Note: Statistically significant difference at the 95% confidence level: Pearson Chi-Square = 21.510, with four degrees of freedom, although three cells (30%) with an Expected Frequency of less than five.
Source: Authors' surveys: Scotland ($n = 215$) and SW England ($n = 51$)

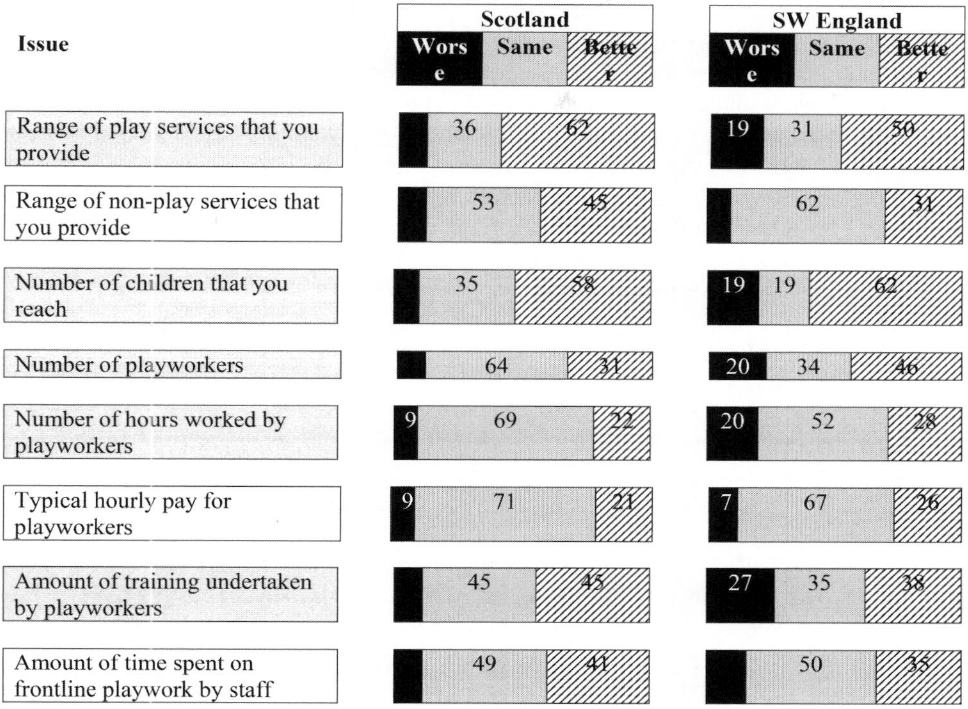

Issue	Scotland			SW England		
	Worse	Same	Better	Worse	Same	Better
Range of play services that you provide	36		62	19	31	50
Range of non-play services that you provide		53	45		62	31
Number of children that you reach		35	58	19	19	62
Number of playworkers		64	31	20	34	46
Number of hours worked by playworkers	9	69	22	20	52	28
Typical hourly pay for playworkers	9	71	21	7	67	26
Amount of training undertaken by playworkers		45	45	27	35	38
Amount of time spent on frontline playwork by staff		49	41		50	35

Figure 4.   Playwork practitioners' evaluation of play in their own play organisation in 2013 for Scotland and SW England. Note: Variable labels in shaded cells denote a statistically significant difference in the results between Scotland and SW England at the 95% confidence level.
Source: Authors' surveys: Scotland ($n = 182$–214) and SW England ($n = 42$–52)

(50% and 62%, respectively); and very few reported that the range of non-play services had worsened (7% and 2%, respectively). Nevertheless, a significant minority of one-fifth of playwork practitioners in SW England reported that both the range of play services provided and the number of children reached had worsened in 2013 (19%) and, for both these issues, playwork practitioners in SW England were more likely to report a more negative experience in 2013. However, it must be acknowledged that, since information was not collected of the number of providers who have stopped delivering services (and it was less likely that the survey would reach playwork practitioners with this experience), even though satisfaction with individual organisations is shown to increase, this may be against a hidden backdrop of overall loss of services and numbers of children reached.

Playwork

Surprisingly, more positivity than negativity was expressed for each of the playwork indicators in SW England (Figure 4). For example, with regard to the number of playworkers in their organisation in 2013, in SW England 46% opined that this had improved, compared to 20% who considered that it has worsened. Indeed, for each of the five playwork conditions on which opinion was canvassed, a significant number of playwork practitioners reported improvements in 2013, with this being a more common experience than matters worsening or staying the same for both the number of playworkers in their organisation and the amount of training undertaken by those playworkers, although this is belied by the tenor of open-ended comments submitted along-side these fixed response survey questions.

In Scotland, playwork practitioners also expressed more positivity than negativity when reflecting on playwork in their organisation in 2013. Typically, fewer than 1 in 10 playwork practitioners in Scotland considered that matters has worsened, for example, only 9% reported that the number of hours worked by playworkers in their organisation has worsened in 2013. It was most common for playwork practitioners in Scotland to report that there has been no change to playwork in their organisation in 2013 (e.g. 71% reported no change to typical hourly pay, although as the cost of living has gone up, this represents a drop in real terms in the value of remuneration for playwork). The most positive response was for training where 45% reported that the amount of training undertaken by playworkers in their organisation (in Scotland) had improved in 2013.

Reflections

In many ways, the experience of play in 2013 differed between playwork practitioners in Scotland and SW England. Statistically significant differences were found for most of the organisational issues, half of the regional issues, and both of the indicators of overall satisfaction. In each instance where a difference was observed, conditions in 2013 had worsened more in SW England than in Scotland. First impressions are that it is problematic to portray a 'global' experience of play in the UK and that the ancedotal and case study evidence contrasting the fortunes of play in England and Scotland in 2013 are acknowledged by, and find expression through, playwork practitioners' reflections on their work.

More generally, 2013 appears to have been a period of flux for play in the UK. Although 'staying the same' was a common response, change is more prevalent. Furthermore, although there are reports of positive change, negative change and no change for all issues, on the whole 2013 was characterised in both Scotland and SW England by much more positive than negative change in playwork practitioners' own organisations (Figure 4), but a more complex mix of positive and negative trends for the region as a whole (Figure 2).

The comparative framework assists in better understanding the broad context of playwork in 2013. Thus, although more playwork practitioners in SW England reported that their overall satisfaction with play in SW England has not worsened (58%) and that their overall satisfaction with play in their own organisation has not worsened (74%), the more positive complexion of these results is checked when set against experiences in Scotland (91% did not report that play in Scotland has worsened in 2013 and 94% did not report that play in their organisation had worsened). In particular, the experience of government differs markedly with local government in SW England far more likely to be thought to be reducing funds for play, and national government far less likely to be thought to have a positive outlook on play. Interestingly, these seem to have had little bearing on how parents and adults in the wider community have regarded play overall, as distinct from services, with playwork practitioners in both Scotland and SW England reporting similar experiences and predominately little change in 2013.

Turning to the substantive foci of the research, there is a strong sense that play capacity has worsened in SW England in 2013; although only the opinion of a significant minority (one in four) that the amount and quality of playspace had worsened, there is a strong sense that support for those who deliver play in communities and the amount of money being invested in play by local authorities has worsened. A substantial proportion of playwork practitioners also thought that local authority investment had been reduced in Scotland, although here there was less evidence of reduced play capacity in terms of playspace and available support.

There was acknowledgement of the loss of skilled playworkers in SW England. Interestingly, observations of playwork in the respondent's own organisation were less negative and, in many instances, more positive than negative. Working conditions, availability of training and pay were reported to have improved or stayed the same on the whole. There is, however, a not insignificant minority of playwork practitioners in SW England who report worsening conditions of service in 2013 (around one in four respondents).

Comments to an open-ended question at the end of the survey personalise the issues and, to a large extent, reinforce the quantitative evidence, with significant differences in tone between respondents in the two regions. The tone of comment from SW England is primarily negative, overwhelmingly opining that lack of funding is adversely affecting the sector, both nationally and in the SW region, where lack of funding for training is particularly highlighted. Absence of a national play strategy and perceived Government indifference is criticised by many, as is a perception that the value of play is not understood, for example:

(There is a) [L]ack of funding available to ensure the continuation of existing high quality provision.
(Playworker and Service Manager, Voluntary sector, provincial city)
(I am) [V]ery concerned that with budget cuts at county level, there will be no funded playwork training.
(Senior Playworker and Trainer, Social Enterprise company)
(There is an) [A]pparent lack of acknowledgment and recognition of the value and importance of play by the Coalition
(Project Officer with Council Play Team, although not delivering play services)
England is letting its children, young people and their families down by not taking play seriously.
(Playworker, Social Enterprise company)

While concerns are also expressed over funding in Scotland, there is widespread appreciation of the potential contained within the Scottish Government's Play Strategy and cautious optimism of a play-friendly cultural change. Reflections on 2013 tended to cover a much wider range of issues than in SW England, and many of them provided detail on very local situations, for example:

Funding from local authorities is reducing, so time is spent accessing other funding, which takes a long time and will impact on services.
(Manager of a voluntary sector play organisation, small town)
The play strategy is excellent and I wholeheartedly agree with its content.
(Local Authority Playworker, in rural area)
There seems to have been a growing understanding among the education and childcare sector that play is an essential part of children's learning.
(Self-employed Forest Schools Practitioner, serving urban and rural areas)

Conclusions

Austerity impacted on play in 2013, but not in a uniform manner. It is too simplistic to boldly assert that austerity is impacting negatively on play and playwork. In SW England, the more strongly negative experience of government (both national and local) in 2013 does not seem to be translating into a negative experience in the workplace, although there may be fewer work-places, which is the case nationally (Joswiak, 2014). In Scotland, the impact of a more supportive national (Scottish) government, must be balanced against the reduction in spending on play by local authorities.

There are several key conclusions that should be drawn from these observations. First, there is merit in adopting a frame of reference for analysing support for play, playwork and the play sector that extends beyond individual regions in the UK. A related point is that care must be taken when utilising evidence that purports to convey collective experience across the four sub-nations of the

UK. Commonality of perspective, experience and priorities cannot be assumed across the UK at the current time. Second, consideration must be given to who speaks for play (or more precisely, who speaks for playworkers or playwork practitioners) in the UK. The discord among the observations in SW England on the wider region (primarily negative) and the workplace (primarily positive) is not necessarily an inconsistency. Rather, it tends to suggests that those who remain in playwork have maintained a positive working environment, but are aware of the wider (and less positive) trends that have impacted on the wider region. There would be merit in attempting to capture the experiences of those exiting the profession (or those less embedded in the profession as a result of casual or seasonal work) if the totality of playworking is to be understood. Finally, the contrasting tenor of the results for workplace and wider region in SW England affirm the importance of holistic appraisals of playwork – focusing only on either the workplace environment, or alternatively on the wider experiences of play in the region, would have cast a very different impression and understanding of playwork in SW England in 2013.

Disclosure statement

No potential conflict of interest was reported by the authors

References

Ferguson, A., Page, A. (2015). Supporting healthy street play on a budget: a winner from every perspective. *International Journal of Play.* doi:10.1080/21594937.2015.1106047

Gove, M. (2010). *Michael gove's letter to directors of children's services.* October 20, 2010. Retrieved November 14, 2013, from https://www.gov.uk/government/publications/revised-play-capital-allocations-for-local-authorities

Gove, M. (2013). *Michael gove speaks about the importance of teaching.* September 13, 2013. Retrieved November 14, 2013, from https://www.gov.uk/government/speeches/michael-gove-speaks-about-the-importance-of-teaching

Hayes, M. (2014). CYP Now investigation: play services decimated as funding slashed. *Child and Young People Now.* January 8, 2014. Retrieved January 10, 2014, from http://www.cypnow.co.uk/cyp/news/1141407/cyp-investigation-play-services-decimated-funding-slashed

Heidenreich, M., & Zeitlin, J. (Eds). (2009). *Changing European employment and welfare regimes: The influence of the open method of coordination on national reforms.* London: Routledge.

Hocker, P. (2014). A play space to beat all. *Journal of Playwork Practice, 1*(1), 104–108.

Joswiak, G. (2012, November 13). Newcastle play services face closure. *Children and Young People Now* Retrieved from http://www.cypnow.co.uk/cyp/news/1075334/newastle-play-services-closure

Joswiak, G. (2014, January 7). Outdoor play under threat from local facilities and funding cull. *Children and Young People Now*. Retrieved from http://www.cypnow.co.uk/cyp/analysis/1141332/outdoor-play-threat-local-facilities-funding-cull

Kane, D., & Allen, J. (2011). *Counting the cuts: The impact of spending cuts on the UK voluntary and community sector*. London: NCVO.

Leith, M., & McPhee, I. (Eds). (2012). *Scottish devolution and social policy: Evidence from the first decade*. Cambridge: Cambridge Scholars.

Martin, C. (2014). Playwork cuts: The effects of austerity on playworkers, playgrounds and play services. *Journal of Playwork Practice, 1*(1), 92–99.

McKendrick, J. H., Kraftl, P., Mills, S., Gregorius. S., & Sykes, G. (2015). Complex geographies of play provision dis/investment across the UK. *International Journal of Play*. doi:10.1080/21594937.2015.1106042

Morton, K. (2012). Camden to close play services, *Nursery World*, January 18, 2012. Retrieved November 7, 2013, from http://www.nurseryworld.co.uk/article/1112784/camden-close-play-services?HAYILC=RELATED

Play England. (2011). *Government to discontinue national play contracts*. February 14, 2011. Retrieved November 15, 2014, from http://www.playengland.org.uk/news/2011/02/government-to-discontinue-national-play-contracts.aspx

Play in Peril. (2013). *The list of cuts, cutbacks and closures so far*. Retrieved November 8, 2013, from http://playinperil.wordpress.com/6-the-list-of-cuts-cutbacks-and-closures-so-far-a-work-in-progress/

Playday. (2010). *Playday 2010 opinion poll summary*. Retrieved November 7, 2013, from http://www.playscotland.org/wp-content/uploads/assets/Playday-2010-opinion-poll-findings-final.pdf

Playday. (n.d). *About playday*. Retrieved November 7, 2013, from http://www.playday.org.uk

Scottish Government. (2013). *Play strategy for Scotland: Our vision*. Edinburgh: Scottish Government. Retrieved November 8, 2013, from http://www.scotland.gov.uk/Resource/0042/00425722.pdf

Skillsactive. (2004). *Playwork people*. London: Author.

Skillsactive. (2006). *Playwork people 2*. London: Author.

Skillsactive. (2008). *Playwork people 3*. London: Author.

Skillsactive. (2010). *Playwork people 4*. London: Author.

UNITE (2013). *The State of Playwork: Survey on Playwork 2013*. Retrieved September 27, 2013, from http://www.uniteforoursociety.org/blog/entry/the-state-of-playwork-survey-on-playwork-2013/

Vasagar, J. (2010). Playground plans shelved under government spending Cuts. *The Guardian*, August 11, 2010. Retrieved November 14, 2013, from http://www.theguardian.com/politics/2010/aug/11/playground-plans-frozen-spending-cuts

Woolley, H. (2015). Slip sliding away: A case study of the impact of public sector cuts on some of the services supporting children's play opportunities in the city of Sheffield in the north of England. *International Journal of Play*. doi:10.1080/21594937.2015.1106045

AUSTERITY AS OPPORTUNITY

Supporting healthy street play on a budget: a winner from every perspective

Alice Ferguson and Angie Page

Street play has declined in recent decades due to increasing traffic and reduced independent mobility [One Poll. (2013). *Playday 2013. Opinion poll summary*. Retrieved December 9, 2013, from http://www.playday.org.uk/playday-campaigns/2013-playful-places/playday-2013-opinion-poll.aspx]. This paper presents two perspectives on how street play can and should be promoted for optimal health in young (and older) people. First, Alice Ferguson, Director of *Playing Out*, a resident-led Community Interest Company based in England, describes the development of a simple, elegant, low-cost approach to opening up streets for play. Second, Angie Page, an academic from the University of Bristol, articulates why grassroots street play projects such as these are important to deliver the challenging public health task of increasing physical activity in young people.

Introduction

Street play has declined in recent decades due to increasing traffic and reduced independent mobility (One Poll, 2013). This paper presents two perspectives on how street play can and should be promoted for optimal health in young (and older) people. First, Alice Ferguson, Director of *Playing Out*, a resident-led Community Interest Company based in England, describes the development of a simple, elegant, low-cost approach to opening up streets for play. Second, Angie Page, an academic from the University of Bristol, articulates why grassroots street play projects such as these are important to deliver the challenging public health task of increasing physical activity in young people.

Birth of a grassroots movement

My neighbour and I set up *Playing Out* as a response to our children's lack of freedom to play independently on their own street. The volunteer-driven model of street play that we have developed helps lay the foundations for outdoor play becoming a normal part of children's everyday lives. As a low-cost intervention, it is also a very attractive means to achieve this in these times of 'austerity'.

We know that the majority of children across the UK do not achieve recommended physical activity levels (Health and Social Care Information Centre, 2013). However, contrary to the predominant media message, parents are not wholly to blame for this. Society as a whole needs to

52

take responsibility for the social and environmental conditions that have limited children's access to outdoor space, particularly our collective 'decision' to give over our cities to motorised transport. *Playing Out* reimagines the street as a public space belonging to all.

Five years ago, I was concerned that my children (then aged 4 and 8) were not getting enough informal play, interaction and physical activity. Simply sending children out to play independently was no longer the norm in my urban residential neighbourhood, as had been the case a generation ago. Getting my children outside involved escorted trips to the park, the woods or other 'safe' spaces, which, even for a parent who had the time, the means and the motivation, just did not happen often enough. My parents' generation did not face this dilemma – as children, we had freedom in the immediate neighbourhood. The street was an extension of home and there was always someone to play out with. In contrast, when my children were younger, our street felt a barren and unwelcoming place, dominated by traffic, which was neither a safe nor appealing place to play. To paraphrase Jane Jacobs, 'nobody enjoys being out on an empty street' (Jacobs, 1961, p. 45).

An annual street party showed us how the street could be temporarily transformed simply through removing cars. However, this involved a collective effort from neighbours to organise food and activities and all parked cars had to be moved from the street. We wanted something simpler and more every day, so we developed the *Playing Out* model – an after-school partial road closure, for a prescribed and limited period of time, organised and stewarded by neighbours, solely for the purpose of providing a safe space for free play.

We initially trialled the idea on International Children's Day 2009. We did nothing other than stop through traffic and asked residents to drive in and out at walking speed. We were really interested to see if children would want to come out or still knew how to play in the street! We did not need to worry – of course they did. This confirmed our instinct that children's urge to play out freely was still intact – they just needed the time, space and permission to do so.

Playing Out, the organisation and movement, grew out of that single event. We helped some other streets locally to do the same thing and then shared all of our learning via a website, making it freely available for anyone across the country to follow or adapt the model (Playing Out, n.d.). *Playing Out* has now become a hub for information, contact, encouragement and advice to others wanting change for their streets and their children. We go out to streets across the city of Bristol in south west England giving hands-on support to residents. We are starting to grow a network of key resident-activators to replicate this model in other places.

The response from parents and others has been positive, with people organising playing out sessions on over 250 streets across 40 different towns and cities in the UK. Reassuringly, in all of these places, we keep finding the same thing – get rid of fast traffic and children come out and play in all kinds of ways – they respond creatively to the space and opportunity to play right outside their homes. Maybe because it is a blank canvas, the street seems to invite more variety of play than is typical in a designed playground. Although not 'hard evidence', it is telling that, during a field visit to our street, Britol City Council's Play Manager asked, 'How did you get the children to engage in so many different play types?' The answer to that question is, 'We didn't, they just do (when afforded the opportunity).'

There is also something about being out on your own street that puts children in contact with other people and 'real life' in a way that differs to that in school, designated playspaces and organised activities. It gives children (and adults) a sense of community, citizenship and belonging in their own neighbourhood. The street where you live is not just a public space – it is *your* space.

Many of those with responsibility for children's health and community development have been supportive. It costs them next to nothing – the main job of the authorities is simply to sanction the activity and allow people to get on with it. Bristol City Council responded to the project by piloting a 'Temporary Play Street Order', an annual licence allowing streets to hold weekly 'playing out' sessions (Bristol City Council, n.d.; Playing Out CIC, 2012). Several other councils have already followed suit and many more are interested.

It is clear to us that many other parents also really want this freedom back for their children and are prepared to take action to make it happen. This grassroots activity, combined with peer-to-peer support and supportive Councils, has helped the *Playing Out* idea to spread, first via word of mouth to neighbouring local streets, then via local media coverage and promotion at community events more widely across the city of Bristol and, latterly through national media coverage across the UK.

From my personal experience I can say that, since the introduction of regular 'playing out' sessions, it is becoming more normal for my children to play out on the street, even when open to cars. As a parent, I certainly feel much more relaxed about letting them be out there unsupervised, as do other parents on the street.

Playing Out is part of wider movement for change and although it can feel like we are 'up against it', what galvanises us all is the fear that our children's health and happiness are seriously at risk if we do not sort this out. There is also a sense of urgency as we may be the last generation of parents who remember when playing out in the street was the norm, and so we are motivated not lose this forever.

Whilst funding cuts are never a good thing, austerity measures can be used as an additional driver to recast play as something that is not wholly reliant on funded 'provision' (although this is certainly necessary as things stand) but rather, a normal part of children's everyday lives, supported and accepted by wider society.

The big picture

The *Playing Out* model that Alice has described is effective as a mechanism to promote physical activity because it allows regular access to active play, close to home, in a space which is free from risk of harm from motorised traffic. Economically, it is attractive as it is a low-cost intervention. The cost or impact on other users, namely drivers, is also minimal because road closures take place at a time when there is little traffic. Residents can also still access the street for parking.

Promoting street play is an important intervention to increase physical activity, which complements the many existing school-based interventions. Whilst school-based interventions can be successful at increasing physical activity, they often have limited impact beyond the school gate (Van Sluijs, McMinn, & Griffin, 2007). The *Playing Out* model promotes neighbourhood active play in the after-school period. The timing is important as this period represents a 'critical window' for maximising physical activity. It is at this time that children (and parents) generally have more choice about how they spend their time and subsequently when differences in activity between those least and most active are often most marked (Page et al., 2005). However, there are few effective interventions to increase physical activity after school. Promoting street play offers a mechanism to address this for the following reasons:

- If we get children to spend more time outdoors than indoors they will be, on average, three times more active (Cooper et al., 2010).
- The greater the proximity of places to play, the more time children will spend outdoors in those places (Active Living Research, 2011).
- Children spend more time outdoors on built surfaces such as streets than they do in green space (Wheeler, Cooper, Page, & Jago, 2010).
- Traffic is a major barrier to parents allowing their children independence to play outdoors (Jago et al., 2009)

- Fostering this independence is an important mechanism to increase physical activity as children age (Page, Cooper, Griew, Davis, & Hillsdon, 2009, 2010).

Resurrecting regular street play therefore may be an important mechanism to increase children's physical activity, even in times of austerity.

Disclosure statement

No potential conflict of interest was reported by the authors.

References

Active Living Research. (2011). *The potential of safe, secure and accessible playgrounds to increase children's physical activity*. Briefing Report.

Bristol City Council. (n.d.). *Road closures for events and street parties*. Retrieved from http://www.bristol. gov.uk/page/transport-and-streets/road-closures-events-and-street-parties#jump-link-9Playing

Cooper, A. R., Page, A. S., Wheeler, B. W., Hillsdon, M., Griew, P. J., & Jago, R. P. (2010). Patterns of GPS measured time outdoors after school and objective physical activity in English children: The PEACH Project. *International Journal of Behavioral Nutrition and Physical Activity*, 7(31). doi:10.1186/1479-5868-7-31

Health and Social Care Information Centre. (2013). *Statistics on obesity, physical activity and diet*. London: Lifestyle Statistics.

Jacobs, J. (1961/1993). *The death and life of Great American Cities*. New York: Modern Library edition.

Jago, R. P., Thompson, J. L., Page, A. S., Brockman, R., Cartwright, K., & Fox, K. R. (2009). Licence to be active: Parental concerns and 10–11-year-old children's ability to be independently physically active. *Journal of Public Health*, 31, 472–477.

One Poll. (2013). *Playday 2013. Opinion poll summary*. Retrieved from http://www.playday.org.uk/playday-campaigns/2013-playful-places/playday-2013-opinion-poll.aspx

Page, A. S., Cooper, A. R., Griew, P. J., Davis, L. H., & Hillsdon, M. (2009). Independent mobility in relation to weekday and weekend physical activity in children aged 10–11 years: The PEACH project. *The International Journal of Behavioral Nutrition and Physical Activity*, 6(2). doi:10.1186/1479-5868-6-2

Page, A. S., Cooper, A. S., Griew, P. J., & Jago, R. (2010). Independent mobility, perceptions of the built environment and children's participation in play, active travel and structured exercise and sport: The PEACH project. *International Journal of Behavioral Nutrition and Physical Activity*, 7(17). doi:10. 1186/1479-5868-7-17

Page, A. S., Cooper, A. R., Stamatakis, E., Foster, L. J., Crowne, E. C., Sabin, M. A., & Shield, J. P. H. (2005). Physical activity patterns in non-obese and obese children assessed using minute-by-minute accelerometry. *International Journal of Obesity*, 29(9), 1070–1076.

Playing Out. (n.d.). *What is it*. Retrieved from http://playingout.net.

Playing Out CIC. (2012). *Bristol's 'temporary street play order' trial September 2011–2012*. Bristol. Retrieved from https://www.bristol.gov.uk/streets-travel/playing-out

Van Sluijs, E., McMinn, A. M., & Griffin, S. J. (2007). Effectiveness of interventions to promote physical activity in children and adolescents: systematic review of controlled trials. *British Medical Journal*, 335, 703.

Wheeler, B. W., Cooper, A. R., Page, A. S., & Jago, R. (2010). Greenspace and children's physical activity: A GPS/GIS analysis of the PEACH project. *Preventive Medicine*, 51(2), 148–152.

AUSTERITY AS OPPORTUNITY

Opportunities for free play

Rob Wheway

Children's freedom to play is more dependent on the public realm (streets, pavements, verges, incidental open space, front gardens) than it is on playgrounds and parks. Children play where road design slows traffic down (street play). Play strategies which concentrate on the provision of play facilities are flawed because increased provision cannot compensate for the reduction in children's freedom to play caused by the domination of the car in residential roads. Current 'Play Streets' legislation needs to be altered so that its purpose is to 'promote a healthy lifestyle and increased neighbourliness'. They should be called 'home roads' or similar so that they cater for the whole community. Such an approach would also help tackle obesity.

Introduction

I have worked in children's play since 1971 and, since 1990 I have regularly carried out observational and interview research of children[1] playing freely in the outdoor environment (including playgrounds, play schemes and adventure playgrounds, where present) in over 70 neighbourhoods in England and Wales. This paper summarises the key findings from that body of work (Children's Play Advisory Service, n.d.; John & Wheway, 2004; Wheway & Millward, 1997).

Insight from Cardiff

My most recent research was for Cardiff City Council where we compared two areas of housing (Wheway, 2011). Area 1 comprised straight roads of terraced housing with a large primary school right in the middle; Area 2 was of cul-de-sac design with roads deliberately designed with bends to slow traffic down. We found significant differences in the numbers of children playing out unsupervised (Table 1). In this context, 'playing out' included children who were independently mobile (walking, cycling, skating, etc.).

The observations were carried out during a cold February half term. Admittedly, these are small numbers. However, they are representative of the observations that I have drawn from many other similar studies in the UK. Whilst not all of the children who were observed would be 'playing' in the strictest definition of that word, the figures indicate how the environment shapes differences in children's freedom to play. Free play depends on independent mobility.

Table 1.   Children's street presence in Cardiff in Winter.

| Area type | Child by age and gender | | | |
	Infant girl	Infant boy	Junior girl	Junior boy
Terraced	0	0	1	3
Cul-de-sac	2	2	24	34

Source: Author's own field observations (Wheway, 2011).
Note: Infant is approximately 4–8 years old; junior is approximately 8–11 years old.

Play location

My research has consistently concluded that location is the most important factor in deciding where children play. Three aspects of location should be considered:

- *Location – Can children get there?* If children cannot get to a place without supervision then they are not freely able to play there. Most public roads are an impenetrable barrier to play for children.
- *Location – Can they 'see and be seen'?* Up to the age of about 10 both children's and their parents' preference is to play in places where they can see and be seen by a trusted adult. This is usually their own parent but it might also be a friend's parent in the next street or a playworker. Even in decades previously when children's ranges were greater than they are now, everyday play places tended to be within sight and sound of home.
- *Location – Is it 'where it's at'?* Children want to play where there is a good chance that they will meet other people (not just children). They want to feel part of what is going on in their neighbourhood. Unfortunately, there is sometimes a tendency to situate children's play facilities 'out of sight and out of mind'. What I have found is that such play areas are much less likely to be used and are more likely to be vandalised and susceptible to other inappropriate activity.

The three locational criteria are also relevant for supervised play facilities. I have seen children ignoring what would be regarded by play professionals as a facility with high play value, and playing instead on a much more modest play environments, such as grass verges and the spaces between garages. The difference is that the 'good' facility did not meet the three locational criteria, in contrast to the less obvious play place.

An important finding from my research is that where children can play out there appears to be more neighbourliness. People talk about 'keeping an eye out' for each other's children.

Play distances

The distance between the place where children actually play and the designated play place may be as little as 50 metres. The distance to children's usual everyday play place is nearly always less than 100 metres.

However, the practice of planners to draw a circle around a play area and call it the 'catchment' is nonsense. It is the travel distance – and not the straight line distance – that matters. Thankfully, Geographic Information System can be used effectively to plot actual travel distances – rather than straight line point-to-point distances.

Even the most cursory glance at a street plan will confirm that there are large areas without public open spaces or playgrounds within 100 metres (travel) of children's homes. The limited

Figure 1.   Typical street space in a UK housing area – at the far end of the street is a road which is too busy for the children to cross.
Source: Author.

play range of children means that for the vast majority of children their local road is the only place where they could be able to play freely.

It is impractical and unrealistic to expect any local authority to knock down houses at regular street corners to provide play facilities. Therefore, the reality is that roads need to be made safe for play – as they are the only place in which many children play. The everyday reality of street play for children (and their parents) is that their local street space is not amenable to play (Figure 1).

We should stop blaming parents for curtailing children's outdoor play and start to focus more attention on addressing environmental design and neighbourhood planning priorities so that they feel it is safe to let their children play out.

Play strategies

For too long decision-makers have audited play facilities on the basis of number of square metres of provision (outputs) rather than whether they improve children's freedom or opportunities to play or not (outcomes) or whether they are even likely to be used by children. The accessibility which is location dependent is ignored. Playgrounds are often centralised in town parks where children can only attend occasionally when their parents are accompanying them. This is not lax parenting. Free play has always been mainly unsupervised. Children do value parents or trusted adults being near enough to run home to.

If we are to redress the decline in children's play opportunities, and facilitate everyday 'free play', our play strategies need to move away from an emphasis on facility provision. We need to concentrate on creating an 'environment for play'. Children's play is more dependent on the public realm (streets, pavements, verges, incidental open space, front gardens) than it is on play-grounds and parks.

The play environment of the street

Help is at hand from legislation enacted during Margaret Thatcher's premiership. In the *Road Traffic Regulation Act* 1984, the provision for roads to be designated 'street playgrounds' was continued (Hocker, 2014; and see Ferguson and Page in this collection). Unlike Home Zones (Gough, n.d.), street playgrounds can be created at very little cost (Figure 2).

Although a well-meaning piece of legislation, the premises upon which it is based are flawed. Firstly, it suggests that the street should be re-envisaged primarily for the benefit of children; whereas, in contrast, it might be argued that the benefits should be to all (adults and children alike) who want to walk, talk, hang out and be active on street space. Secondly, the legislation suggests that the street is a facility, rather than an opportunity. This is an important distinction to draw with regard to auditing facilities, for if streets are facilities it negates the need for existing play provision, or safe routes to it. Finally, the legislation implies that children from miles around will descend on that which is designated a 'street playground'. Were this to be realised, then it would be likely that the designation of the 'street playground' would be vociferously opposed by some residents.

The same legislation could be used more effectively if the title was changed to 'home roads', 'safe streets' or something similar, and the purpose was refocused to 'promote a healthy lifestyle and increased neighbourliness'. Such a reorientation would not only broaden the range of beneficiaries and therefore be more popular and less threatening, but would still give children the same improved environment.

Not only would the changing of the street designation give back to children the play opportunities which have been lost since the 1970s, other benefits which accrue, many of which are likely to be attractive to funders and political decision-makers, i.e. tackling obesity; increasing neighbourliness (consistent with ideas of the Big Society); improved Olympic Legacy of increasing fitness; and less burning of fossil fuel (as it would become quicker to walk shorter distances, rather than navigate to street playgrounds).

We have promoted the child's right to play for decades (UNCRC, 2013) and yet children's freedom to play has decreased year on year. The problem is we have tended to concentrate on the right of a few children to play in high-quality facilities. The budget restrictions of the 'era of austerity' may inadvertently afford an opportunity for the play sector in the UK to refocus attention on what matters most – the development of rich everyday environments for children's play.

Figure 2.   Street playground in London, ca. 1950s.
Source: London Play.

Disclosure statement

No potential conflict of interest was reported by the author.

Note

1. In my research in observations and interviews I have included all those who appear to be engaged in a 'playful' activity. The senior age group has been taken as being approximately 10 to approximately 15. As far as travel distances go, there is a significant change at about 10 or 11. At 11 parents have to let their children to secondary school unaccompanied and so having allowed that they allow them to go further afield for play and other recreational activities. Parents seem to start letting go of the reins at about age 10 when the inevitability of secondary school is imminent. In my findings there is a really significant difference between 9 and 10 year olds whereas the difference between 7 or 8 and 9 year olds is not much. So the specifics in that section are up to approximately 10 year olds.

References

Children's Play Advisory Service. (n.d.). *Publications*. Retrieved November 18, 2013, from http://www. childrensplayadvisoryservice.org.uk/publications.html.

Gough, N. (n.d.). *Typical measures and their cost*. Retrieved November 18, 2013, from http://www. homezones.org/measures.html.

Hocker, P. (2014). A play space to beat all. *Journal of Playwork Practice, 1*(1), 104–108.

John, A., & Wheway, R. (2004). *Can play, will play: Disabled children and access to outdoor playgrounds*. London: Fields in Trust. Retrieved November 18, 2013, from http://fieldsintrust.org/Upload/Documents/ Products/can_play_will_play_1004006374.pdf.

Road Traffic Regulation Act. (1984). Retrieved November 18, 2013, from http://www.legislation.gov.uk/ ukpga/1984/27/contents.

UNCRC. (2013). *General comment no. 17 (2013) on the Right of the Child to Rest, Leisure, Play, Recreational Activities, Cultural Life and the Arts (art. 31)*. Retrieved November 18, 2013, from http://www2.ohchr.org/english/bodies/crc/comments.htm.

Wheway, R. (2011, July 4). *Most play strategies are wrong*. Paper presented at the International Play Association conference, Cardiff. Retrieved November 18, 2013, from http://www.playwales.org.uk/ login/uploaded/documents/Events/IPA%202011/rob%20wheway.pdf.

Wheway, R., & Millward, A. (1997). *Child's play: Facilitating play on housing estates*. York: JRF. Retrieved November 18, 2013, from http://www.jrf.org.uk/sites/files/jrf/1900396262.pdf.

RETHINKING PLAY AND SOCIETY

Promoting playfulness in publicly initiated scientific research: for and beyond times of crisis

Cindy Regalado

Playfulness facilitates the introduction of new concepts and ideas and thus breaks down barriers to full participation with otherwise 'intimidating' tools or spaces. We inevitably engage in play when (co)developing technologies and initiating collective research. Through case studies of 'playshops' I here show that playfulness provides an engaged setting for learning through curiosity and wonderment but also through embracing mistakes as a way to overcome the fear of exploring and welcoming new outcomes. This is especially true when engaging in scientific exploration using Do-It-Yourself tools and methodologies. Our role as facilitators and educators is to tap the potential of people to engage in civic science with a playful component.

On playfulness

The overlap between my academic and public work is both theoretical and practical. On the one hand, it is about understanding how people envision and devise methods as well as create, re-purpose, and use technologies that enable them to apply their civic capacities in scientific research initiatives that help them explore, challenge, and/or question the state of things. On the other, my work is about (co)creating the spaces and opportunities, rhetoric, and practices that demystify engagement with science and technology, invite curiosity, and promote playfulness and the joy of understanding and engaging with the world on our own terms.

I define playfulness as an inviting, attentive, and disarming attitude, based on Hans (1981). This attitude, as Gordon (2010, p. 15) elaborates, provides an exploratory drive in which 'we leap out of constraints in order to obtain freedom, we leap for joy to celebrate achieving freedom, and we leap across frames because we are free to explore'. As we shall see in the next section, we inevitably engage in play when initiating collective research and (co)developing technologies. In some cases, playfulness facilitates the introduction of new concepts and ideas and thus breaks down barriers to full participation with otherwise 'intimidating' tools or spaces (Figure 1). In others, it provides an engaged setting for learning through curiosity and wonderment. Playful interactions can also provide the potential to overcome the obstacles imposed by perceptual barriers of knowledge and expertise. This is especially true when engaging in scientific

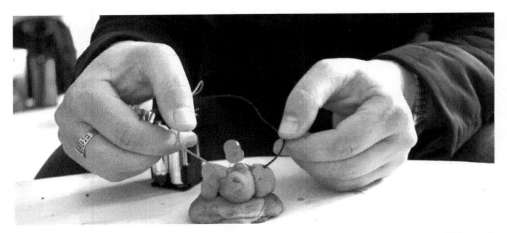

Figure 1.   Building 'squishy circuits' at the Touch|Play|Learn mini-Expo, an initiative at the Mildmay Community Centre in London. Salt and sugar-based home-made play-dough functions as conducting and insulating material [Photo: Cindy Regalado].

exploration using Do-It-Yourself (DIY) tools and methodologies. In our activities thus far we have observed that a DIY approach to research involves an attitude of 'throwing off constraint', that is, detaching 'messages, experiences, or objects from their context of origin, creating a new

Figure 2.   Teens at the Hyperion Lyceum School in Amsterdam (a) created head-box prototypes (b) using DIY *Public Lab* techniques to modify cameras (c) and by repurposing materials such as cardboard boxes (d) that then allow passers-by to experience the world as if they could see near infrared light (e) [Photo courtesy of Jeffrey Warren and Cindy Regalado].

frame that allows for greater freedom, interactivity, and creative possibilities' (Millar, 1968 in Gordon, 2010), as seen in Figure 2.

Case study: the playful nature of 'Science has no Borders'

Science has no Borders (ScHNB) began in early 2012 with University College London support to assist people who are usually not involved in research to start their own investigative projects. It aims at engaging people not as passive participants but as 'community researchers' who investigate an issue of concern to them by building and using their own investigative tools – whether these be spectrometers or sculptures – to ask and potentially answer different questions about their social, natural and built environment. ScHNB activites include 'Touch|Play|Learn' and the playshops 'Exploring borders through Art', 'Explorer of the world', and more recently 'For the Love of Mess'. These are briefly described below.

Touch|Play|Learn

There are many DIY tools and techniques available, prototyped by citizens to address issues of interest or concern to them, as was the case in the Gulf of Mexico, where a group of community organisers used DIY kite and balloon mapping to engage with their communities in collecting imagery to show, with high-definition aerial photography, the extent and exact location of the damage of the BP oil spill (Bourne, 2010; Shkabatur, 2014). This collective action gave rise to the non-profit *Public Laboratory for Open Technology and Science* (Public Lab) in 2010.

Groups such as *Public Lab* have dedicated much of their efforts to developing and promoting 'civic science' as a way to question the state of things, using affordable and locally sourced tools with DIY techniques (Public Lab, n.d.). These tools and techniques form a collection of resources that communities can use, re-purpose, and develop further to suit their needs, whether it is for serious leisure or for advocacy and environmental justice.

Touch|Play|Learn was a mini-Expo, held in 2012 at the Mildmay Community Centre in East London to engage with local residents and showcase resources such as those of *Public Lab* and other DIY investigative tools. Visitors were invited to touch the tools, play with them, and investigate ways in which they could learn about themselves and their surrounding environment (Figure 3).

It was through play that local residents got involved; children came and through play, they learnt not only about DIY tools (circuits, LED lights, and about how sound and thermal sensors work) but also about abstract concepts such as temperature differences and how we define noise pollution. The children then brought their parents and kindled in them an interest in DIY tools as well. These were immigrant families; some parents did not speak English but their children did and they acted as facilitators for their parents. The children taught their parents and the parents began to touch, to play, to learn, and to trust in their abilities.

'Explorer of the world' playshops

Continuing with the idea of presenting, prototyping, and sharing DIY tools and techniques we planned and deployed five free-of-charge and fully hands-on activities of public engagement during August and September 2013, with the last four led by two members of *Public Lab*, Shannon Dosemagen and Mathew Lippincott. The first workshop introduced DIY aerial photography using kites, where members of the public learned about its applications and flew kites with cameras attached to the kite lines, as seen in Figure 4.

Figure 3.   The Touch|Play|Learn was an initiative at the Mildmay Community Centre where local residents were invited to touch the DIY prototype tools, play with them and try them out, and in doing so, learn about how they can learn about themselves and their surrounding environment [Photo courtesy of Helga Hejny].

In the second workshop, Shannon and Mathew led a kite-making session in which we learnt how to make our own delta kites out of locally sourced, affordable materials (Figure 5).

The third workshop involved flying DIY kites to capture aerial imagery over Clissold Park in Hackney, East London. We learnt about the uses of composite aerial imagery and used the online *Public Lab* open-source software MapKnitter.org to make our own composite aerial photo of the park. The fourth and fifth workshops were dedicated to DIY Spectrometry, where we learnt about the basics of spectrometry, spectral analysis, and its application in environmental monitoring and everyday sensing. The fifth and last workshop involved learning to use the open-source online software SpectralWorkBench.org to calibrate the DIY spectrometers and test the variation in spectral signatures for different substances, such as branded and store-branded soda (Figure 6).

'Exploring borders through art' playshops

With a focus on 'interactions with ourselves' and exploring who we are, we developed a series of four playshops using artistic expression as a way of channelling thoughts and feelings in an experiential and visual way. The artwork created offered a way to reflect on and challenge our state of mind and conceptions about the world. In the first playshop, 'Cloodle', we created an artwork in 2D and used it to explore and challenge how our sense of identity is active in the way we perceive ourselves and conceive the world; in 'Sensosketch', we explored and challenged how our senses influence observation of the world around us, using repurposed tactile material to create 3D artwork; in 'Sculptorade', we explored and challenged how our imagination functions, and how we choose and make sense of our experiences by making our own puppets (Figure 7); and in 'Juxtallage', with the aim of bringing it all together, we co-created ways of expressing ourselves and knowing each other by using our physical selves in artistic expression (Figure 8).

Figure 4.   Introducing kite-mapping in London. Using a DIY kite, we introduced the concept of DIY aerial photography. (a) Assembling the DIY kite, 'Barney', hand-made from 'Tyvek' at the Public Lab annual Barnraising event in Louisiana, US. (b) Members of the group Citizens without Borders take turns reeling out kite line. (c) Aerial photograph captured by a camera attached to the kite; the camera is set to continuous shooting. The aerial photo shows algal blooms in a lake in southern UK, mid-June [Photos: Cindy Regalado].

In this final playshop, led by Sarah Palette (co-founder of Vagrant Muses), we juxtaposed and merged the physical representations we created from disparate stimuli (pictures, poems, and quotes). The end result was a powerful act telling the story of how we relate to the world. The key in Juxtallage was to practise a lack of expectation, appreciating things for what they are, and getting back to a child-like state of playfulness and wonderment. In all the playshops, we kept a record of our multiple thoughts, interpretations, reflections, and observations throughout the sessions.

'For the love of mess'

There is no such thing as a failed experiment, only experiments with unexpected outcomes. – Buckminister Fuller (Parry, 1997)

Firestein reminds us that we should embrace ignorance and failure because they are the true drivers of education and research – it is this 'not knowing' and 'not understanding' that 'gets

Figure 5. Kite-making workshop with the Public Laboratory for Open Technology and Science. The materials used are affordable and locally sourced. 'I can definitely see the power of DIY!' [Photo: Cindy Regalado].

researchers into the lab early and keeps them there late' (2012, p. 4). Following the tradition of previous playshops, in this series I invited attendees to embark on an exploratory journey to redefine their relationship with 'failure' by purposefully making mistakes and embracing them as experiments or as new ways of trying things. The series was born out of the previous playshops, 'Exploring Borders through Art' and 'Explorer of the World' to directly come to terms with the fear of trying something new, experimenting, admitting failure, and acknowledging ignorance as part of the process of learning. Through the five sessions of the 'For the Love of Mess' playshops series took 'experimenters' through basic and playful non-judgemental experimentation ('Rippity' and 'Creorama') to then give representation to their relationship with 'messing up' and 'mistakes' ('Visualudio'). For the fourth playshop, 'Locuria', we left the enclosed and 'safe' environment provided by the workshop classrooms (akin to a laboratory) and tested our experiences in 'the real' outside world. This involved engaging in acts of giving to strangers – such as 'free hugs', 'free friendly chat', or 'free story'. Preparation for this last experiment included Brown's (2010) talk on 'The power of vulnerability'. Experimenters made and decorated their own signs and a 'support group' stood nearby for safety and to cheer the 'experimenter' as they engaged in their act of giving. Reflections on experiments from these playshops revealed a breakthrough in personal trust, as the comments on the playshop webpage show:

> It was very daunting at first, but then thoroughly enjoyable and truly did lift my spirits! I felt part of a community not only with the group, but with the strangers we engaged with on the street!
> It felt like going through that trust test thing (throwing ourselves in the net of entwined arms of others). Instead, this time we are throwing ourselves in complete strangers' arms. Afterwards, I felt warm inside.

Figure 6. Testing the Public Laboratory DIY Spectrometer. In the final workshop, we tested samples of soda and wine using the open-source software SpectralWorkBench.org. The first step in using the tool is to calibrate it using compact fluorescent light [Photos: Cindy Regalado].

Took me a while to be inspired with something I wanted to give to strangers, eventually I came up with a pleasing gift(s). Encouraged by seeing Grace[1] throw herself into the experience, I did too and was uplifted, enlivened, stimulated and intrigued by breaking through another border. I'm sure the life enhancing results of this experiment will prompt me on a daily basis to repeat it.

The closing playshop, 'A serious case of … ', drew from the art of improvisation theatre to consolidate the learning from all of the playshop experiences: working together to create meaning and overcoming the fear of exploring and welcoming new outcomes – essential to publicly initiated scientific research. A comment in the playshop webpage encapsulates this:

Thanks to all for making these playshops possible especially Cindy for putting together a diverse, fun filled package which was facilitated with panache. I was tickled, enthralled and challenged in a most encouraging way, which enlivened my parts of me which were somewhat dormant. It was kwazee fun to spot a new species, which we named A Happypottymuss.

Final thoughts

Flying kites and balloons for aerial photography (Figures 4 and 9) engages people in ways often not considered; the quote in Figure 9, by a member of *Public Lab* illustrates this. Publicly initiated

Figure 7. Exploring borders through art: artwork created in a series of playshops to interact with ourselves and explore who we are through artistic expression and reflection [Photos: Cindy Regalado].

Figure 8. Juxtallage: bringing it all together to create a new grammar of artistic expression across social and cultural borders of understanding [Photo: courtesy of Ted Fjallman].

scientific research should not only arise out of necessity (a crisis or due to a lack of support from authorities) but also as an ideal way we engage in research creating new ways of knowing and understanding, of exploring and doing, of tapping into our potential, of giving rise to unheard voices, and embracing mistakes as part of the process of learning. As Gertz and Justo (2012) argue, understanding brings knowledge and with knowledge comes the power to make decisions that can change our lives for the better – from holding polluters accountable, campaigning to lower electricity and gas bills, to getting to know ourselves again for the first time! Through our work we have proved that playfulness is a very important attitude that aids in the process of building capacity and (self-)trust. Our role as facilitators and educators is to tap the potential of people to address issues that are important to them; to acknowledge and push for a belief in people – in their abilities, their skills, their passions, and their knowledges; which at the moment is highly undervalued and underestimated.

Play is a key component in our work at *Citizens Without Borders*: engaging with individuals and groups through play it is not only the way we learn but it also builds memories and experiences harnessed in enjoyment for doing something close at heart; it makes us feel a part of something greater. When engaging with DIY technologies and engaging in DIY research there is a very powerful element at work – there is genuine joy when learning that you are able to do, sense, or create something you did not think you could, especially, when you have made the invisible visible with your own hands. Playfulness embodies a sense of 'involvement and detachment, self-expression and self-transcendence, individuality and cooperation' (Gordon, 2010, 14). Boundaries become fluid, defences dissolve, and give way to spontaneity. I believe that it is in this context and with this attitude that exploration and experimentation for discovery in publicly initiated scientific research can be kindled.

It is important to continue research on this because many people are already taking initiative in solving their own problems, they are ingenious and resourceful, imaginative and creative – and

Figure 9.   The role of 'play' in flying kites and balloons for aerial photography. Balloon mapping in Birmingham, UK [Photo: Cindy Regalado].

they know the power that knowledge can bring. Through my work with communities in the UK, Mexico, and other parts of the world I have learnt the humble lesson that our role, from within academic institutions, needs to move to that of facilitators to give impetus and guidance to their initiative-taking.

Disclosure statement

No potential conflict of interest was reported by the author.

Note

1.   The name of the participant has been changed to protect privacy.

References

Bourne, J. K. (2010). Is another deepwater disaster inevitable? *National Geographic* October. Retrieved November 7, 2013, from http://ngm.nationalgeographic.com/2010/10/gulf-oil-spill/bourne-text

Brown, B. (2010). The power of vulnerability. Retrieved November 7, 2013, from http://www.ted.com/talks/brene_brown_on_vulnerability

Firestein, S. (2012). *Ignorance: How it drives science*. New York, NY: Oxford University Press.

Gertz, E., & Justo, P. D. (2012). *Environmental monitoring with Arduino: Building simple devices to collect data about the world around us*. Sebastopol, CA: O'Reilly Media.

Gordon, G. (2010). What is play? In search of a universal definition. iP-Dip, 148: 11–20. Retrieved November 7, 2013, from http://cyps.northyorks.gov.uk/CHttpHandler.ashx?id=24082&p=0

Hans, J. S. (1981). *The play of the world*. Amherst, MA: University of Massachusetts Press.

Millar, S. (1968). *The psychology of play*. Harmondsworth: Penguin Books.

Parry, M. (Ed.). (1997). *Chambers biographical dictionary*. Edinburgh: Larousse.

Public Lab. (n.d.). *About Public Lab*. Retrieved November 7, 2013, from http://publiclab.org/about

Shkabatur, J. (2014). Interactive community mapping: Between empowerment and effectiveness. In G. Björn-Sören & B. Savita (Eds.), *Closing the feedback loop: Can technology bridge the accountability gap?* (pp. 71–106). Washington, DC: The World Bank.

RETHINKING PLAY AND SOCIETY

'Strategic playwork': a possibility that is neither 'intervention playwork' nor 'environmental playwork'

Arthur Battram 🆔

In the 1970s, playwork was part of a broad, enriching perspective that focused on 'the whole child'. While acknowledging that change is accelerating, bringing with it greater complexity, we still tend to search for simplistic order. The so-called 'age of austerity' in which we find ourselves is a contemporary attempt to impose order on the chaos that is the global economy. The search for order is pertinent to many aspects of play in contemporary childhood. It is the child of the immensely influential paradigm of modernity and the resurgence since the 1970s of neo-liberal capitalism and advanced liberal politics. At a time of growing insecurity, dislocation and insecurity generated by these forms of liberalism, the narrative claims to offer certainty and redemption. One consequence of this push for order is to increase chaos in the complex system that is our globalised world, and the nature of 'complexity' is explained. The crucial aspect of systems in this state, known as 'complex adaptive systems' is that we cannot control them, we can only influence them. Because control of a complex system (or more precisely, a complex adaptive system) is not possible, attempting to control will have negative consequences. Thus is created precarity, a condition of existence without predictability or security, affecting material or psychological welfare. Two flawed approaches to playwork can be discerned: Intervention playwork – the provision in times of plenty of a resource-intensive enclave in which to herd children in order to protect them, and Environmental playwork – an approach which looks at the barriers that prevent children from playing in their communities and attempts to mitigate them in a variety of ways. A third longer-term approach to the development of play is required that can respond quickly to its changing environment, yet be grounded within a long-term perspective. A complex approach that takes a strategic and long-term perspective, whilst encouraging experimentation and learning at the level of community provision. The Welsh approach is described as a strategic perspective which places a duty on local authorities to assess and secure sufficient play opportunities for children in their area. That which is loved will persist, like a drystone wall maintained by generations.

The lost world

In the 1970s, playwork was part of a broad, enriching perspective that focused on 'the whole child': an approach epitomised by The Plowden Report (Central Advisory Council for Education, 1967), Summerhill School (n.d.), adventure playgrounds and the Home Office's Community

Development Programme (Smith, 2006). These times were characterised by an unashamedly progressive social programme for a society with a still-functioning welfare state and largely affordable public housing. Four decades on, one might argue that playworkers are the poor relation of the children's workforce, with playwork considered to be equally deliverable by part-time poorly paid childcare staff, as by qualified playwork staff (on account of both holding a Level Three award in the framework for vocational qualifications). More broadly, social programmes now struggle to address, never mind ameliorate, socio-economic inequalities. The world has changed.

Thinking about society: not simple, not complicated, but complex

Regrettably, for the most part, our understanding of the world has not changed. While acknowledging that change is accelerating, bringing with it greater complexity, we still tend to search for simplistic order. The so-called 'age of austerity' in which we find ourselves is a contemporary attempt to impose order on the chaos that is the global economy. The search for order is pertinent to many aspects of play in contemporary childhood. In the words of Peter Moss, when reflecting on the prevailing approach to early childhood:

> It is the child of the immensely influential paradigm of modernity and the resurgence since the 1970s of neo-liberal capitalism and advanced liberal politics. At a time of growing insecurity, dislocation and insecurity generated by these forms of liberalism, the narrative claims to offer certainty and redemption. (Moss 2007)

Similarly, Anthony Elliot, reflecting on Ulrich Beck's 'risk society' (Beck, 1992), a theory that is pertinent to debates on childhood safety and outdoor play, reflects that it is:

> ... bound up with the development of instrumental rational control, which the process of modernisation promotes in all spheres of life – from individual risk of accidents and illnesses to export risks and risks of war (Elliott, 2009, p. 285, this author's emphasis).

Paradoxically, one consequence of this push for order is to increase chaos in the complex system that is our globalised world, and we will need to look at the nature of 'complexity' to understand why. We need to unpack this: firstly by explaining what we mean by a complex system. As is explained in more detail in Battram (1998), since the time of the Ancient Greeks, science has been aware of three system states: (I) Stasis, (II) order and (III) chaos. Recently Complexity Science has identified a fourth state (IV) complexity, which exists in between order and chaos. The crucial aspect of systems in this state, known as 'complex adaptive systems', is that we cannot control them, we can only influence them. They possess only 'bounded predictability'; they contain elements of both order and chaos – they exist at 'the edge of chaos' in 'the zone of complexity' – they are emergent self-organising phenomena which come into being as a result of *bottom-up interactions* between the myriad components of the system (Battram, 1998). Crutchfield (2009) eloquently delineates the complexity of our world:

> The world economy, financial markets, air transportation, pandemic disease spread, climate change, and insect-driven deforestation are examples of truly complex systems: They consist of multiple components, each component active in different domains and structured in its own right, interconnected in ways that lead to emergent collective behaviours and spontaneous architectural reorganisation.
>
> This is the world we built. Nation states maintain their survival and enhance their well being by participating in international trade. The degree of participation reflects the strength of coupling their internal economies to the external world – the extent being a choice that balances internal needs

and externally derived benefits. International trade is managed, in turn, at the largest scale via govern-mental negotiation, trade organisations, and global finance firms who rely on inter-connected national markets. Internally, each state's financial system consists of a number of players, from national reserve and investment banks to insurance companies, institutional investors, mortgage banks, asset-based banks, and workers. The real-economic component – materially productive industries and services – is supported by land, ocean, and air transportation systems. And this synopsis is only one slice. It says nothing of human culture and politics. The more one attempts to describe the social environ-ment and technological systems we have constructed, the more complex they appear and the larger the mystery of their functioning becomes.

How are we to begin to understand truly complex systems and their hidden fragilities? Unfortunately, when it comes to considering how complex systems should be designed and should function, contem-porary science and engineering, in their traditional positive and constructive role, largely miss the emergence of fragility. (p. 4)

Because control of a complex system (or more precisely, a complex adaptive system) is not possible, attempting to control will have negative consequences. Thus is created *precarity*, a con-dition of existence without predictability or security, affecting material or psychological welfare, which is affecting increasing numbers of people globally: zero hours contracts, supermarket sup-plier switching, movement of work to non-unionised low-pay economies and so on. We can see precarity as a consequence, as the outcome, of attempted *control* – based on a *false* perception that order and predictability are being lost to increasing chaos. As our society moves in a state of com-plexity, attempts by corporations and governments to create islands of order result in an increase in chaos in the surrounding wider society. Think of the vast mass of ordered Health and Safety and Child Protection procedures which are failing to protect children from harm.

The attempt to control is a failure of perception, the result of thinking with the simplistic tool of either/or logic. We fail to see the complexity that exists at the boundary between order and chaos. Thus, we leap to simple solutions, ignoring the wise words of Oliver Wendell Holmes Jr (1841–1935), 'I would not give a fig for the simplicity this side of complexity, but I would give my life for the simplicity on the other side of complexity.' Complex problems demand complex thinking: hence Conrad Waddington's *Tools for Thought* (1977) or Ivan Illich's *Tools for Conviviality* (1973). Simple solutions tend to generate further problems, for instance the dis-astrous effects of the introduction of cane toads into Australia to control pests (Australian Gov-ernment, 2009). Each 'simple' solution leading to another 'simple' problem, never engaging with the underlying complexity.

Binary thinking in playwork

When we look at child-rearing, and drawing on the thinking of Hurst (2002), we can observe that two broad approaches can be adopted: on the one hand, children herded into an enclave for their own safety, to be raised by experts. On the other, children are left to their own devices and are perceived to be com-petent to be an integral part of society (Harris, 1999). Jacobs (1961) describes this latter approach in action: 'non-matriarchy environment for children to play' in a loose community. We can characterise this as children roaming in a 'contested multi-functional space' (the street), which takes shared respon-sibility for them (the casual overseeing of the social 'rough and tumble' of life on the street). In this view, children are seen as 'legitimate peripheral participants' (Lave & Wenger, 1991) in the life of a community and are accepted as an integral part of society: they have a right to be there just as anyone else does. We can clearly see these two perspectives at play within playwork:

- *Intervention playwork* – the provision in times of plenty of a resource-intensive enclave in which to herd children in order to protect them. This approach is exemplified by the adventure playground. The playful invasion of an impoverished high street or shopping centre by 'Pop-up Play Shops' (Jozwiak, 2012) is another example.

- *Environmental playwork* – an approach which looks at the barriers that prevent children from playing in their communities and attempts to mitigate them in a variety of ways, such as structural changes to the physical environment, and/or the provision of activities such as 'street play' as a way of re-colonising the outside as a legitimate play environment. One notable example is Bristol's 'Playing Out': a parent-led project which temporarily closes a street to traffic to allow children to play (see Ferguson and Page, in this collection).

But, both approaches are flawed: how are children to make their way to an enclave of play provision if there is not a play-friendly and child-friendly environment through which to navigate? Equally, how can children take part in challenging activities, if they are perceived by adults to be dangerous and a nuisance? *Playing Out* has already seen resistance from neighbours alarmed that an occasional special event might become part of everyday life (Ferguson, 2013).

Based on my own experience, the *Whitworth Park* 'youth shelter' is one example of such failure. A local campaigner succeeded in raising funds for somewhere for young people to congregate in Matlock. Unfortunately, the shelter that was provided was both inhospitable (having no walls because of adult fears of encouraging inappropriate behaviour out-of-sight) and wrongly positioned (well away from already frequented play areas 'for younger children'). The initiative failed because its approach was based on fear and myths about young people, who still visit the park, preferring to sit on the steps of the Whitworth centre. When I pointed out the shelter to a group of teenagers, they did not know what it was.

Space only permits one positive example: the Venture is based in one of the most deprived estates in Wales, Caia Park in Wrexham. It was, the model for Integrated Children's Centres across Wales. The project has grown and developed over almost 40 years, almost two generations. The most effective playgrounds have grown to become embedded in their communities and there is no better evidence of this than the fact that several of the children who used to use the Venture are now employed there as staff.

Systemic playwork: navigating complexity for tomorrow's playwork

A much broader, longer-term approach to the development of play is required; this approach must stand outside the whims of central government funding. Such an approach might be termed 'Systemic Playwork'. To quote Mulgan (2005), ex-head of Tony Blair's Innovation Unit:

Politicians over-estimate what can be achieved in the short term, and underestimate what can be achieved in the longer term.

Systemic Playwork would focus on learning and experimentation. It would take a humble, piecemeal approach to development. Paradoxically, it could respond quickly to its changing environment, yet be grounded within a long-term perspective. Of necessity, this will require interdisciplinary work rather than, as is usually the case, play being seen as the responsibility of a single underfunded service. A complex approach is needed that takes a strategic and long-term perspective, whilst encouraging experimentation and learning at the level of community provision – what Moss and Petrie (2002) call a 'critical pragmatism':

Vulgar pragmatism holds that a conception is to be tested by its practical effects … what is true and valued is what works in terms of what exists. […] Critical pragmatism continually involves making epistemological, ethical and aesthetic choices and translating them into discourses-practices. Criticisms and judgements about good and bad, beautiful and ugly and truth and falsity are made in the context of our communities and our attempts to build them anew. (Cherryholmes, 1988, p. 179; quoted in Moss & Petrie, 2002, p. 12)

In Wales, a strategic perspective is embodied in Section 11 of the Children and Families Measure 2010 (Welsh Assembly Government, 2010) which places a duty on local authorities to assess and secure sufficient play opportunities for children in their area. This 'Play Sufficiency Duty' forms part of the Welsh Government's anti-poverty agenda which recognises that children can have a poverty of experience, opportunity and aspiration, and that the poverty of play can affect children from all backgrounds.

The long-term success of The Venture in Wrexham (Brown, 2007) can be attributed to the sustained political action of its founder, Malcolm King, who has been Councillor for the area, Leader of Wrexham Council and Chair of the North Wales Police Authority and of the Association of Chief Police Officers community leadership group. Like many adventure playgrounds, it was established in the late 1970s: unlike many it persists today. In a different context, Glamis Adventure Playground in London's Docklands is a rare example of a project resurrected by community demand (Shadwell Community Project, n.d.). On their website they list 35 sponsors, supporters and funders, and this diversity of funding is one key factor in its persistence, the other being love. That which is loved will persist, like a drystone wall maintained by generations.

Disclosure statement

No potential conflict of interest was reported by the author.

ORCID

Arthur Battram ⓘ http://orcid.org/0000-0002-0064-8179

References

Australian Government. Department of Environment, Water, Heritage and the Arts. (2009). *Australian government policy on cane toads*. Commonwealth of Australia.

Battram, A. (1998). *Navigating complexity: The essential guide to complexity theory in business and management*. The Industrial Society.

Beck, U. (1992). *Risk society: Towards a new modernity*. London: Sage.

Brown, F. (2007). *The venture: A case study of an adventure playground*. Cardiff: Play Wales.

Central Advisory Council for Education. (1967). *Children and their primary schools* (The Plowden Report). Retrieved November 18, 2013, from http://www.educationengland.org.uk/documents/plowden/

Cherryholmes, C. H. (1988). *Power and criticism. Post-structural investigations in education*. New York: Teachers' College Press.

Crutchfield, J. P. (2009). *The hidden fragility of complex systems: Consequences of change, changing consequences*. SFI Working Paper. Santa Fe: Santa Fe Institute.

Elliott, A. (2009). *Contemporary social theory: An introduction*. London: Routledge.

Ferguson, A. (2013). Personal Communication to Author, May 24, 2013.

Harris, J. R. (1999). *The nurture assumption: Why children turn out the way they do*. London: Bloomsbury Press.

Hurst, D. K. (2002). *Crisis & renewal: Meeting the challenge of organizational change*. Watertown: Harvard Business Review Press.

Illich, I. (1973). *Tools for conviviality*. New York: Harper & Row.

Jacobs, J. (1961). *The death and life of great American Cities*. New York: Random House.

Jozwiak, G. (2012). *Pop-up shops to address London's play deficit. Children and young people now, October 30, 2012.* Retrieved November 18, 2013, from http://www.cypnow.co.uk/cyp/news/1075141/pop-shops-tackle-london-s-play-space-deficit

Lave, J., & Wenger, E. (1991). *Situated learning. Legitimate peripheral participation.* Cambridge: University of Cambridge Press.

Moss, P. (2007). *Bringing politics into the nursery: Early childhood education as a democratic practice.* The Hague: Bernard van Leer Foundation.

Moss, P., & Petrie, P. (2002). *From children's services to children's spaces: Public policy, children and childhood.* London: Routledge.

Mulgan, G. (2005). Lessons of power. *Prospect Magazine,* May 21, 2005. Retrieved November 18, 2013, from http://www.prospectmagazine.co.uk/magazine/lessonsofpower/

Shadwell Community Project. (n.d.). *About us.* Retrieved November 18, 2013, from http://www.shadwellcommunityproject.org/wordpress/

Smith, M. K. (2006). *Community work.* Retrieved November 18, 2013, from http://www.infed.org/community/b-comwrk.htm

Summerhill School. (n.d.). *Introduction to summerhill.* Retrieved November 18, 2013, from http://www.summerhillschool.co.uk/pages/index.html

Waddington, C. H. (1977). *Tools for thought.* St Albans: Paladin.

Welsh Assembly Government. (2010). *Children and families (Wales) measure 2010.* Retrieved November 18, 2013, from http://www.legislation.gov.uk/mwa/2010/1/contents

CONCLUSION

Geographies for play in austere times

John H. McKendrick, Peter Kraftl, Sarah Mills, Stefanie Gregorius and Grace Sykes

This concluding essay to a collection of 10 papers examining, *Best of times to worst of times? Appraising the changing landscape of play in the UK*, reviews six key themes that emerge – re-fuelling longstanding tensions within playwork; organisational legacy of the investment years; broad acceptance of the wider value of play in society; the need to develop a critical play intelligence within the sector; the reconfiguration of play geographies and the impact of play provision on local play cultures; and the need for a much more central focus on play cultures in our enquiry. Without question, Austerity has undermined the public investment in play and play services that characterised the UK in early years of the Millennium. Nevertheless, for every 'threat' that this poses, others are able and willing to conceptualise this as an opportunity to reprioritise play priorities. It is argued that play is resilient, and adept an adapting to the changing realities of the financial landscape.

Tensions eased, tensions raised: play in contemporary UK

Tim Gill describes the recent history of play in England as a 'rollercoaster'. This analogy has merit, and was the premise that gave rise to the seminar in Leicester, from which this collection of papers was derived. As Tim's paper details, and the others in this collection each suggest, the UK Government's commitment to children's play, unparalleled levels of investment, a strengthened national and regional play leadership, professionalisation of the playwork workforce (Skillsactive, 2010), and an ever more expansive evidence base to extol its value, took play to the top of the hill, only for post-austerity cuts to bring it right back down again.

Although the facts of the matter cannot be disputed, how these facts are to be regarded are open to multiple interpretations. It is perhaps the litmus test for whether a UK playworker is an optimist or a pessimist to ask their opinion of the recent history of play in the UK; the former will emphasise the progress made in the growth years and the legacy it has left behind; while the latter will bemoan the potential not realised of an English National Play Strategy (DCSF & DCMS, 2008) and on-going disinvestment from play through local funding cuts. Some of the cuts, as Helen Woolley recounts in Sheffield, are a subtle scaling back of provision (such as the reduced opening hours at the Highfields Adventure Playground and the diversion away from playwork of the Rangers), while others are an unequivocal withdrawal of resource (such as the rationalisation of Sure Start centres).

What seems readily apparent from this collection of papers is that the new realities of play in times of austerity in the UK have brought to the fore a range of tensions that may have been supressed, or marginalised, in the era of investment. Although Tim Gill observes that the play sector became better at projecting a united front to its paymasters, some fundamental differences of opinion were never far away. Arthur Battram discusses one such issue – the choice between interventionist playwork (provision of resource-intensive environments that, as Alexandra Long and Tim Gill both recount, were the focus of much recent investment) and environmental playwork (the concern to dismantle barriers, such as transforming the street into a playspace that is championed by Alice Ferguson and Angie Page). Arthur seeks a third way, what he describes as strategic playwork, a holistic yet piecemeal approach that seeks the transformation of local culture to accommodate play. Rob Wheway is not averse to capitalising on opportunities that present through the scaling back of interventionist playwork investment; however, rather than promote 'street play', he would instead champion 'free play'. Without prejudicing through description either position as a problem, this might be conceived as a tension between the pragmatists (street play) and the fundamentalists (free play). Similar simmering tensions are evident between those who are primarily concerned to demonstrate the value of play for the attainment of a wide range of social goals and those who are more concerned to promote the inherent value of play. Alexandra Long's observation of the failure of the play sector to use the Best Play 'Play Objectives' (NPFA, Children's Play Council and Playlink, 2000) as a framework to evaluate the impact of Big Lottery funded play projects, may be lamented and regretted by those who value play for its own sake. Then again, as Alexandra herself notes, there are already differences of opinion over whether play should be evaluated in terms of outcomes achieved or merely on facilitating access to play opportunities (which, in turn, would allow such outcomes to be achieved). Perhaps this highlights a crisis in the definition of play without which we may struggle to move forward in a united fashion. Or perhaps it simply highlights the need for increased collaboration and cross communication across play organisations, academia and local authorities to collate evidence and present powerful arguments for the importance of play. If so, there is a need to work together to ensure that children have access to play facilties whether this be purpose built infrastructure or the re-imaging and transformation of everyday spaces regardless of the differing reasons as to 'why' we think play is important.

Legacy of the 'investment years'

Has, as Tim Gill suggests, the status of play plummeted in the UK? In the introductory note to this collection, we also referred to the derisory (and ill-informed) comments of the UK Minister with responsibility for play (Gove, 2013) and suggested that this may be indicative of play not being accorded the value that it warrants in Government, and beyond.

As noted above, Alexandra Long expresses concern that the sector has not grasped the opportunity to evidence the positive value of play. Although there is some evidence of new play infrastructure being laid to waste in the austerity cuts (Morton, 2011), there is no national understanding of whether this infrastructure persists as a positive physical legacy of the investment years; whether sustaining this infrastructure has been to the detriment of wider play provision; or whether the infrastructure has been allowed to fall. With more certainty, although Play England is a much smaller organisation after the cuts, it is without question a much stronger organisation than before the investment and one that provides much stronger support for play having benefited from it; the same can also be said of Play Scotland, Play Wales and Playboard

NI. Although Tim Gill is concerned at the falling status of play, one legacy that persists from the early challenge of the UK Government to 'speak with a strong united voice' is that there is now much evidence of play fulfilling a role as a valuable ally to others.

Play in service of society

Some might worry that too much attention is paid to demonstrating the utility of play to achieving others' socially desirable goals, and that this endeavour might be at the expense of promoting the inherent value of play. Whether desirable or not, furthering alliances beyond play have had value to fend off the worst excesses of the 'austerity cuts', supporting those whose livelihood depends on play to sustain employment. Alliances have been forged across departments in local authorities (as Helen Woolley outlines for Sheffield) and across Third Sector organisations (as Tim Gill describes for Play England). The play sector continues to be skilled at demonstrating the wide range of benefits that can accrue from play and, as a result, secures money to support the on-going development of play (Conway, 2014).

Although we might question the sincerity of Government support for play, or indeed the level of understanding of the value of play in the claims that are made for it, across the UK play has been utilised as an integral part of key national social strategies. Tim Gill explains how the desire to respond to a very poor ranking on UNICEF's study of child well-being in rich nations (UNICEF, 2007) led to the UK Government investing more significant sums in play than the sector had envisaged. The Scottish Government's second annual review of progress on their *Child Poverty Strategy for Scotland* (Scottish Government, 2013) makes explicit reference to money invested in play through the *Go Play* and *Go 2 Play* programmes of Inspiring Scotland (Inspiring Scotland, 2013), as an element of its anti-poverty strategy. An even more explicit articulation of the role of children's play in combatting child poverty has been articulated in Wales (Play Wales, n.d.). Play is valued for more than its play value and that is an opportunity upon which play can, does and should, capitalise.

Play intelligence

The utilisation of evidence to inform, or appraise, policy has a long history. In the 1990s, there was an intensification of evidence-based policy in the UK as the then Government sought to disassociate itself from interventions that were grounded in ideology, in preference for an approach that was defined by 'what works' (Boaz, Grayson, Levitt, & Solesbury, 2008). In this context, Tim Gill's recollection of the challenge made by Chris Smith to articulate the value of play should come as no surprise, even if, as Tim suggests, the same Government Minister was already aware of the positive impact of play on children's lives in Islington (London).

Through *Best Play*, the play sector met the challenge set by the UK Government (NPFA, Children's Play Council and Playlink, 2000). However, as Alexandra Long argues, it later fell short of demonstrating positive impact from the investment that followed. At times, evidence has worked against play; Helen Woolley reports how the community of the Pitsmoor Adventure Playground were poorly served by evidence that failed to account for the wider impact of the service it provided. At other times, evidence has worked for play; it was noted above how the UNICEF study of child well-being (UNCEF, 2007) was a catalyst for further investment through the *Play Strategy*. The play sector has also embraced evidence; Play Scotland has developed a toolkit through which local authorities and community groups can self-assess whether they 'provide sufficient play opportunities in terms of quantity and quality' (Play Scotland, n.d.) and SkillsActive completed four annual surveys to better understand the character of the playwork workforce between 2003 and 2009 (Skillsactive, 2010).

What this clearly demonstrates is the need for the capacity within the play sector to generate, interpret and utilise evidence in support of play. Although not beyond the capabilities of playworkers (e.g. Smith, 2014), particularly when rich qualitative insight is valued as evidence from reflective practitioners, it does add another capacity to the desirable skill set of playworkers. Or, as this collection demonstrates, the need for playworkers to foster fruitful alliances with academia. Chris Martin's work with John McKendrick in this collection, may be an example of what can be achieved when the insight of playwork practitioners is brought together with the research expertise of academics. Although evidence alone is not a guarantor against disinvestment, and although powerful allies are needed among decision-makers (as Tim Gill recalls of his time engaging with Chris Smith), evidence can be a powerful ally.

There is also a need to conceive of evidence in the form of 'play intelligence', rather than merely 'information about play'. The sector was correct to warmly welcome the unprecedented £235 million of investment in children's play that was promised (if not delivered) through the DCSF's National Play Strategy in 2008. However, shared among over 11 million children in England (aged under 18), and spread over a three year period, this amounts to a little over £7 per child per year, or about 2p per child, per day; hardly a sum to transform the play fortunes of children in England. Even if we allowed that this investment was only to support the play of children aged 4–11 years old, it would still only amount to 4.5p per day over this three year period. What these calculations demonstrate is that there is a need for play data to be scrutinised and interpreted intelligently. While much would have been achieved with the sum of £235 million that was originally allocated for England's *Play Strategy*, critical analysis of the figures is needed to demonstrate the folly of over-stating its potential. More than ever in these leaner times, what is needed is play intelligence, rather than more information about play.

Reconfiguring the geographies of playspace provision and decision-making

Notwithstanding the limits to its transformative potential, the scaling back of the investment through the *Play Strategy* has generated uncertainty as to its geographical impact, across a range of contexts and geographical scales. What is clearer is that there are two dominant forces at work at the current time in the UK that are working toward alternative geographical outcomes. On one hand, as Helen Woolley recounts in Sheffield, there is rationalisation of play services and play facilities that is leading to less visible public landscapes, and material infrastructures, of play. Helen and Rob Wheway also note that this invisibility of public playspace has often exacerbated the peripheral siting of playspaces, to meet the misguided aim of preventing conflict or consternation at the perceived disruptiveness of play. Austerity cuts are giving impetus to this trend. On the other hand, there are pressures to recover everyday environments as playspaces, epitomised in the grassroots initiatives to reclaim the street as playspace (Alice Ferguson and Angie Page) and the desire of Rob Wheway to promote more 'free play', or in the thinking of Arthur Battram, to develop a play culture in which the everyday environment is valued and harnessed for the playspace opportunities it affords.

It is conceivable that the landscape of UK play provision will become a patchwork comprising localities with less visible commitment to playspace, while others have more visible commitment to playspace, at least for certain times within the week. Moving forward, the key issue is less of a concern to map the locational geography of play facilities; rather, it should be to focus on whether different implications follow from environments in which play provision is (i) embedded and omnipresent; (ii) segregated, by time and/or place; and (iii) absent in the landscape. The key geographical challenge that lies ahead is to articulate the impact of play provision on local play culture(s).

The highs that preceded the lows in England (as described by Tim Gill) were not quite as high in Wales, Scotland and Northern Ireland. Play has enjoyed a longer period of commitment from the Welsh Assembly Government, although the levels of investment have fallen far short of that enjoyed in England. In Scotland and Northern Ireland, devolved Government support for play has co-incided with austerity cuts to local Government provision. It may be more accurate in these parts of the UK to suggest that national support for play is, to a degree, off-setting local cuts that are being meted out at the current time. Indeed, at the macro-geographical level, John McKendrick and Chris Martin illustrate how playworkers' in SW England and Scotland in 2013 sense a very different context for play in their respective regions. There is now a complex play landscape in the UK. This complexity may prove to be a safeguard against the marginalisation of play. In the same manner that the Open Method of Co-ordination has been used in the EU to encourage different national Governments to adopt best practice in tackling child poverty (as nations are motivated not to be the least innovative and poorest performing) (Heidenreich & Zeitlin, 2009), so divergent pathways of play development and investment across the national regions in the UK might be used to 'drive up' standards. Equally, in these years of disinvestment from the UK Government, there may be political capital to be gained by devolved Governments of a different political hue adopting a more pro-play stance and positioning themselves squarely against the UK Government (Leith & McPhee, 2012).

Important as these national influences are, what lies ahead may be a less prominent role for both Central and Devolved Governments in the immediate future of play, at least in England. This return to 'localism' creates both opportunities and threats (Woolvin, & Hardill, 2013). As Helen Woolley demonstrates in Sheffield, where local decision-making must be made under challenging fiscal conditions, communities are pitted against each other as they seek to protect their playspace and/or become 'investment-ready' in bidding for limited funding. On the other hand, allowing local people a greater say in determining the nature of their local worlds, has created a political environment that is, at least on temporary bases, conducive to the street play 'movement'. As for the geographies of provision, the shift to 'localism' also makes for greater complexity in play decision-making, it is, for instance, not without significance that the street play movement has drawn upon national play organisations and local academic partners to achieve its aims. This shift to localism may even throw up new possibilties for play; as Cindy Regalado outlines, 'playfulness' is an approach that engages adults and children, and facilitates their participation in action research to address local issues.

Play cultures as our primary narrative

As Alexandra Long, Tim Gill and Helen Woolley all indicate, articulating the impact of play was the focus for much of the 'investment years'. As with many project evaluations, this tends toward reductionist thinking, where the goal is to isolate the specific impact of a play intervention. Outcomes are the end goal, outputs are the deliverables through which these outcomes are achieved, and inputs are the mechanisms for effecting change – all of which are focused on specific play interventions. This compartmentalisation is consistent with an approach to play that is based on 'environmental playwork' and, perhaps even more so for 'intervention playwork'.

As Alexandra Long implores, Play UK must be able to 'talk the talk' if it is to secure funding for play. This need not, however, be the sum total of our concern to evidence the value of play. We must appreciate their competence in understanding their current situation, as 'experts in their own lives' (Cahill & Cahill, 2007), and therefore key players in this process. If Arthur Battram's 'strategic playwork' is a goal worthy of pursuit, then there needs to be a much stronger evidence base than there is at present to extol its value. Playworkers with their capacity to engage children clearly have the potential to work with them as co-producers of knowledge on play. Other challenges in articulating these play cultures must be faced. As Colin Ward articulated in his insight into the anarchic character of some everyday play (Ward, 1978) and as Holloway and Valentine (2000) describe in their conceptualisation of the 'tribal child' as a means of understanding social studies of childhood, if these local play cultures are to be understood as something other than adult interpretations, then there are methodological and ethical challenges ahead. There remains much scope for a more fruitful partnership between play professionals and academics to better understand – in partnership with children – the everyday cultures of play. Once again, as Cindy Regalado suggests, there may even be a more leading role for 'play' in shaping how these engagements take shape.

Concluding thoughts

The starting point for the Leicester seminar was to question to what extent play was suffering from the 'austerity cuts' of the current UK Coalition administration. Each paper in this collection, although to varying degrees, acknowledges the challenges presented, and potential opportunities afforded, for play. Unlike in Scotland, and to a lesser extent Northern Ireland and Wales, these cuts in England have not been offset by a devolved Government that is outwardly supportive of play; on the contrary, the Government with responsibility in England has disinvested, failed to support, and demonstrated some hostility toward play. It would be remiss to ignore that these are trying times for playworkers (McKendrick, Horton, Kraftl, & Else, 2014) and play in the UK.

However, this pivotal historical moment for play in the UK demands more than lament and reactionary responses. Opportunities to reclaim play environments are being grasped (Alice Ferguson and Angie Page's street play). Play UK needs to re-articulate a future vision – be this promoting local play-oriented cultures as Arthur Battram would favour; championing 'free play' as Rob Wheway would favour; or positing play as everyone's ally – families, communities, practitioners and policy-makers alike. Presumably, it will be a vision of a play mix, rather than one wedded to a particular view.

The reality is that funding will not come easy, and may not return for a decade or more. However, play in the UK must be ready when it does return to articulate evidenced argument, as Alexandra Long and Tim Gill suggest, and this involves the need for play practitioners to embrace evaluation as part of their professional competencies (Smith, 2014). It may also be critical that play practitioners find allies across the professional child, youth and education disciplines, in forging more powerful, hopeful cross-disciplinary visions of childhood (Kraftl, 2013). Certainly, despite lean times, third sector organisations like the National Trust (2013) – in their 'Natural Childhood' initiative – have been able to join forces with major partners such as the NHS to offer a compelling, if rather nostalgic, case for outdoor play, education and exploration. Times may be tough, but in these and other ways, it is incumbent of the play sector to lay the foundations for the sector to capitalise on opportunities that lie further ahead.

Disclosure statement

No potential conflict of interest was reported by the authors.

References

Boaz, A., Grayson, L., Levitt, R., & Solesbury, W. (2008). Does evidence-based policy work? Learning from the UK experience. *Evidence and Policy*, *4*(2), 233–253.

Cahill, C. (2007). Doing research with young people: Participatory research and the rituals of collective work. *Children's Geographies*, *5*(3), 297–312.

Conway, M. (2014). The thin of it – Surviving and thriving in austerity. *Journal of Playwork Practice*, *1*(1), 87–91.

Department for Children, Schools and Families and Department for Culture, Media and Sport. (2008). *The Play Strategy*. London.

Gove, M. (2013). *Michael Gove speaks about the importance of teaching. September 13, 2013*. Retrieved November 14, 2013, from https://www.gov.uk/government/speeches/michael-gove-speaks-about-the-importance-of-teaching

Heidenreich, M., & Zeitlin, J. (Eds.). (2009). *Changing European employment and welfare regimes: The influence of the open method of coordination on national reforms*. London: Routledge.

Holloway, S., & Valentine, G. (2000). Spatiality and the new social studies of childhood. *Sociology*, *34*(4), 763–783.

Inspiring Scotland. (2013). *Go 2 Play*. Retrieved November 22, 2013, from http://www.inspiringscotland.org.uk/our-funds/go-2-play

Kraftl, P. (2013). *Geographies of alternative education: Diverse learning spaces for children and young people*. Bristol: Policy Press.

Leith, M., & McPhee, I. (Eds.). (2012). *Scottish devolution and social policy: Evidence from the first decade*. Cambridge: Cambridge Scholars.

McKendrick, J., Horton, J., Kraftl, P., & Else, P. (2014). Space for playwork in times of Austerity? *Journal of Playwork Practice*, *1*(1), 61–99.

Morton, K. (2011). Cuts to children's playgrounds revealed. *Nursery World*, July 12, 2011. Retrieved November 22, 2013, from http://www.nurseryworld.co.uk/nursery-world/news/1105481/cuts-childrens-playgrounds-revealed

National Trust. (2013). *Natural childhood*. Retrieved November 26, 2013, from http://www.nationaltrust.org.uk/what-we-do/big-issues/nature-and-outdoors/natural-childhood

NPFA, Children's Play Council and Playlink. (2000). *Best Play: What play provision should do for children*.

Play Scotland. (n.d.). *Getting it right for play. A toolkit to assess and improve local play opportunities*. Roslin. Retrieved November 22, 2013, from http://www.playscotland.org/getting-it-right-for-play/

Play Wales. (n.d.). *Play sufficiency.* Retrieved November 8, 2013, from http://www.playwales.org.uk/eng/sufficiency

Scottish Government. (2013). *Annual report for child poverty strategy for Scotland 2013.* Edinburgh.

SkillsActive. (2010). *Playwork people 4.* London: SkillsActive.

Smith, H. (2014). Prospects for participatory research on wellbeing with playworkers and children at play. *Journal of Playwork Practice, 1*(1), 108–113.

UNICEF. (2007). *Child poverty in perspective: An overview of child well-being in rich countries. A comprehensive assessment of the lives and well-being of children and adolescents in the economically advanced nations.* UNICEF Innocenti Research Centre Report Card 7. Florence. Retrieved November 15, 2013, from http://www.unicef-irc.org/publications/pdf/rc7_eng.pdf

Ward, C. (1978). *Child in the city.* London: Architectural Press.

Woolvin, M., & Hardill, I. (2013). Localism, voluntarism and devolution: Experiences, opportunities and challenges in a changing policy context. *Local Economy, 28*(3), 275–290.

Sharing playwork identities: research across the UK's field of playwork

Sylwyn Guilbaud

Playwork is a field orientated around and responsive to the play of children. Playworkers recognise the vital importance of children's experiences, which perhaps often, as adults, they cannot fully comprehend. It seems that such valuing of the unknowable permeates many aspects of a playworker's self-identity. However, a discernible tension can be seen between such arguably integral vocational disposition and the processes of distillation and abstraction necessary to professional representation of playwork within theory, text and policy, which also forms the core of playwork curriculum. This paper describes the journey of a research project nurturing and supporting playwork students in their own discoveries of playwork identity, working with raw, unedited, unfixed explorations of self-contributed by recognised playwork theorists and practicing playworkers across the field.

This paper is concerned with the nature of identity felt and expressed by playworkers. The body of discussion will draw on research undertaken with recognised playwork theorists and practicing playworkers across the field. The aim of this initial work with established playworkers was towards nurturing and supporting playwork students in their own explorations of playwork identity. This paper describes the journey of that project, offering particular insight as to the qualities of personal self which playworkers identify as being fundamentally integrated into their practice and sense of being a playworker.

Identity formation is a vast and extensively studied construct, being of foundational concern across the social sciences (Schwartz, Luyckx, & Vignoles, 2011; Wetherell, 2010). Though the threads of self can be teased apart by the focus of an inquiry and its situation within a discipline, the connectivity between such broad delineators as gender, ethnicity, sexuality, occupation, religion, etc., is composite to identity – for synthesis and wholeness seem to be the very requirement of this sense of who we are (Erikson, 1963; Erikson, 1980; Kroger & Marcia, 2011; Schwartz et al., 2011).

A questioning of individual's sense of themselves in the field of playwork is necessarily situated in all the elements of life which can and have been distilled into the paradigms considered fundamental to the formation of vocational identity.

Had the scope of the inquiry, which informs this paper been larger and should, as is the aim, further participation with the research occur, it would be interesting to explore how orientation towards playwork interacts with established theoretical perspectives. How, for example, does affinity with the myriad flexibilities of play, juxtapose with Erikson's suggestion that:

> Identity formation begins where the usefulness of multiple identification ends. It arises from the selective repudiation and mutual assimilation of childhood identifications and their absorption in new configuration. (Erikson, 1980, p. 122)

How does the experience of discovering playwork sit in regard to Weber's view of vocational calling:

> 'Vocation is both active and passive – one must freely give oneself to that which calls one, which by the acknowledgement of that call appears as and becomes one's own. As a free act, vocation is thus defining of the person; as a necessary act, it is expressive of the person. Vocational activity has as itself nothing of the instrumental; it is an end in itself (thus in some sense moral) but without reference to any grounding or act other than the freely chosen commitment of individuals to their own particular fates'. (Weber, Owen, Strong, & Livingstone, 2004, p. xiii)

Furthermore, how might the recognised interplay between cultural situation and vocational calling, within the current climate of austerity's impact on play services, be interestingly explored through the reflective dialogues within the playwork field and with regard to the motivation of playwork students?

Such considerations would be interestingly contextualised in relation to Henricks' (2015) triangular model (see Figure 1).

Henricks differentiates play from other forms of behaviour, arguing 'that play is perhaps the greatest example of ascending meaning, a process people follow to determine the character of what is occurring and then assess the significance of those occurrences' (p. 75). He suggests that play behaviours encourage people to open up to the possibilities of meaning both '*within*

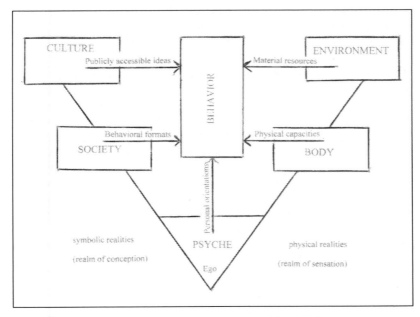

Figure 1.   Fields-of-relationships as frames for behaviour (Henricks, 2015).

events and *beyond events*' (Henricks' 2015, original emphasis). It might be possible to consider the reflection of the rebellious nature of play behaviours in terms of the fields of body, society, environment, and culture, (discussed by Henricks) in relation to the unconventional, somewhat anarchic expressions of self by playworkers and to question the intersection between the formative role of play in self-governance and flexibility, with an identification with freedom and liminality as also discussed by Spariosu (1989, 2013). Towards the construction of such an analytical frame one might, for example, employ Henricks (2015) view that 'within the psyche, playful consciousness (represented by the ego) seeks to destabilise selected psychobiological and psychocultural formations, patterns that stand *above* it in the figure' (p. 76 original emphasis).

However the initial framing of the inquiry sits counter to the unavoidable *focusing in* of any such contextualised lenses. The frame, both in the instigation of the research, and more deeply in response to the nature of what was communicated and how; is composed of the unknowable, the indefinite changeable contradictions, the pauses and shared lost threads at the end of sentences that probe heartfelt experience for a moment's awareness. It is true that this exploration could be comfortably situated within the broad bounds of Narrative Inquiry. It is also important to note that playworkers find meanings and validation for their way of being by borrowing and employing diverse perspectives[1]. Yet, while wishing to avoid all preciousness and convolution, which would in every way be out of step, it is integral to recognise this particular frame as being formed out of the communications of playworkers that resist capture. The impetus was to involve playworker students with the complex human richness that is reflexively intertwined with what is evident in the more polished, edited, presented forms within the field's body of work. Though inseparable from what is overtly visible, the filigree earthy roots are only hinted at by what is above ground. These hints are present, repeatedly throughout playwork texts, they indicate that from which they came and in their distilled form are themselves incomplete; reifications of the unknowing, uncertain, exploratory dialogues of playworkers.

Contextualising the ground – illustrating the hidden and the seeking for 'what we are' in playwork texts

Perhaps the most beautiful published expression of the dichotomy which many playworkers face with awareness is given by Davy (2007 p. 45) 'Playwork, like play, should rightly be process-driven, difficult to define and experimental and should not be overly prescribed or constrained. Try to pin it down, and, like a captured butterfly, it dies.' This is the recognition with which Davy closes the discussion of a chapter which she opens with a questioning as to whether the sector should indeed be trying to define itself, or whether such striving to state its principles and core values is tantamount to 'flapping into, rather than flying away from the butterfly nets?' (Davy, 2007, p. 41).

While the delicate tone of accepted unknowing that occurs in playworker conversations, will always escape the edited page, the urge to provide ourselves with tools which reflect our way seems to take us further from the communication of our responsive flexibility, even when that is what we are stating. This is most apparent when wording initially situated within detailed description becomes deployed and coined.

In the conclusion of a chapter of stories of children playing within a Montessori Nursery, Fisher (2008) describes her way of being, which to me as a reader, had been tangible in her telling of the playing. She writes of her pliability and of going with the flow of play, and tells us that that which is at the heart of her understanding of playwork can be expressed through what Keats calls 'Negative Capability' quoting 'when a man is capable of being in uncertainties, mysteries, doubts, without any irritable reaching after facts and reason' (Keats, 1817, in Fisher, 2008, p. 178). In this same publication Brown (2008) cites Fisher's expression of Negative

Capability in his proposal of the *fundamentals of playwork*, and it is perhaps this very citation which positions 'Negative Capability' into playwork terminology. However while this citation can be seen to illustrate the resonance which Fisher's description held for Brown it also demonstrates the process of abstraction, for already within the context of Brown's chapter, the rewording of Fisher's identification seems to communicate a little less her original.

In 2001 Hughes reuses his IMEE protocol for reflective practice put forward in 1996a. He reminds the reader of its meaning and use as a 'tool for playworkers to organise their analysis of the quality of play environments' (Hughes, 2001, p. 22) using their own Intuitive judgements, their childhood Memories, their professional Expertise and the Evidence they have found in literature. However though the acronym is introduced briefly his illustrative description is rich and complex, he avails the reader of his inner discourse, including his disquiet – 'I have noticed even with "good" playworkers, how great is the qualitative chasm between what they experienced as children themselves and what they are prepared to accept for the children they serve' (Hughes, 2001, p. 26). However one cannot help but wonder whether as it is distilled into its shorthand form and goes out into the world in the playwork toolbox IMEE carries or stimulates a similar unfixed complexity. It seems doubtful, for example, that those accessing this term in *Playwork Voices* (Russell et al. 2007), a publication celebrating the work of Bob Hughes and Gordon Sturrock, written by colleagues in the profession, would glean a sense of its practice. While within this context an assumption of familiarity with the originals is clearly made by the contributing authors, the lack of reflexive texture is nonetheless impoverishing.

There is an undeniable need for language through which the Playwork field can communicate itself, and this is stated as motivation for development of the fundamental playwork theories (Brown, 1989; Brown, 2003; Hughes, 1996b; Hughes, 2006; Sturrock & Else, 1998). To that end the term 'adulteration' put forward by Sturrock and Else within the Play Cycle of their infamous Colorado paper (1998), signifies a position which sets the sector apart from many others who work with and for children. However the recognition that 'There is a danger that the play aims and objects of the children become contaminated by either the wishes of the adult in an urge to "teach" or "educate", simply to dominate, or by the worker's own unplayed out material' (Sturrock & Else, 1998) and the requirement to guard against such 'adulteration' that is taken forward from the paper (Farrow, Stevens, & Stanley, 2003; Davy & Gallagher, 2006; Kilvington & Wood, 2010; Newstead, 2004) cannot encapsulate the diverse subtle moment by moment self-effacing responsiveness of the playworker present in the periphery of playing children. The re-framing of such complexity into a decree of 'thou shalt not' requires for integrity, a contextualisation in the practice orientated self-questioning of each playworker. Seath (2013) provides just such a self-revealing exploration, within which he explains 'this is what I mean when I ask if it's play-healthy: it's not so easy to differentiate if you're taking over the play or not if the child is buzzing along with it too. It's worth repeating again and again that children's play is not about you. *Your* play is *your* play'. However, Seath, with an acceptance of 'heresy', also suggests that 'perhaps … children are sometimes actively seeking adult play ideas by way of their involvement'.

Perhaps this aspect of incompleteness, the reliance of our terms on the playworker's own experience to become enlivened, is itself representative of the dichotomous tension of unknowing and communicable identity (Davy, 2007; Else, 2008; Hanscomb & Virdi, 2007; Melville, 2007; Taylor, 2008). As I have previously proposed this situation 'leaves open the possibility for meanings to be read into seemingly abstracted parts of concepts' (Guilbaud, 2011, p. 59). Such enlivening can be found to happen in the mulling over of our minds and in conversations between playworkers. Here the terms are discussed and stretched, but also rendered somewhat secondary to the detail of the play being wondered at. In our playwork writing this process seems most represented in stories, within which it is sometimes possible to notice that our tangible attempting to express what we sense in truest detail, carries the tone of that which remains unsayable. In the introduction to the collection of '101 Stories of Children Playing' contributed from playworkers, Brown (2014) expresses this situation when he reflects on a story retold by one playworker from another and the accompanying questioning of meaning. He writes 'The meaning of the story (and most of the other stories in the book) is highly ambiguous; it is full of paradox and mystery, which has to be accepted and talked about. It would obviously be possible to analyse this in terms of the SPICE model (Brown, 2003) or play types (Hughes, 2006), but that would be to undervalue the true significance for the child of what's going on' (Brown, 2014, p. 7). While in a recent blog post Seath (2015) adds context to the experienced nuance of writing and also reading playwork stories as he shares his 'thinking on how our playwork stories of play are told and what might lie beneath these tellings', proposing that: 'How we write suggests not only the way our senses absorb the information of the play around and running through us but also the affect that that play has on us' (original emphasis). Though both theory and story in their published form reflect and draw forth different aspects of 'what lies beneath' their incompleteness is integral, as constrained by the necessities of comprehension but also perhaps most authentically by the position of the play-worker in response to play. That which is presented relies, in its coming to be written and perhaps in the deep reading thereof, on experiences of the underground wellspring, the digestive earth of growth and decay, it is the nurturing of this nature of playwork identity that was the motivation for the inquiry.

Methodology of this inquiry

The study set out to involve two sets of participant, namely, up to 20 playwork professionals from the field, and the enrolled cohort of second year playwork students from Leeds Beckett University. Voluntary participants from the playwork field were recruited via an article in the weekly playwork publication iP-D!P (Guilbaud, 2014). This initial invitation described the study and offered a number of open-ended questions to act as an instigating frame for responses.

- How do you understand yourself to be a playworker?
- When you are communicating about playwork with others, where in your body do you feel your conviction, your passion, your uncertainty, your questioning?
- What is your experience of negative capability?
- Do you play with unknowingness?
- What was your last 'wow' play moment when you were not working, and how did it affect you?
- Is there a relationship between your playfulness and creativity and your playwork?
- What else?

In recognition of the non-linear nature of identity, reflection, play and playwork itself, participants were invited to respond either to the questions specifically or to the their own sense of the subject matter, using any means they felt appropriate; be that conversation, written response or creative exploration.

Eleven participants became involved in this part of the study including, playwork authors, adventure playground workers, playworkers in other settings, university lecturers, and those no longer working within the profession but identifying themselves as playworkers. An additional five playworkers were interested in participating but withdrew due to time constraints.

The data from these participants were contributed in the following way: Two face to face interviews, lasting several hours each; two Skype interviews of over an hour each; one written conversation, using social media and email over several weeks; three artistic contributions using words patterns and sketches; three written responses using the questions as a framework. These responses from the playwork field were to be offered to second year playwork students at Leeds Beckett University in such as way as to support their own exploration of playwork identity.

It was recognised in the catalyst for this inquiry at the outset and confirmed by the depth and detail of playworker's self-revealing, that the richness which this data from the field could offer the playwork students was in its very otherness to that which becomes distilled by the nature of analysis and sanitised reification so hard to avoid in the process of representation of a profession in publications and other forms of representation. This position reflected the negative capability, appropriated from Keats by Fisher (2008) and adopted by the field as means of expressing a way of unknowingness, in-expertise and subversion of the conventional child/adult dynamic. There was a challenging imperative that these qualities of negative capability, diversely present in every aspect of the inquiry thus far, be reflected in my bridging of the data to the students.

In order to do justice to what had been given by these individuals in the playwork field it seemed to me necessary to find a means of offering it to the playwork students which communicated the sense of awe that I had felt at the entrustment of such self-revealing material. To this end it seemed vital to communicate what people had expressed in all its raw detail, rather than a condensed interpretation of themes – for to take an abstractive approach would have been contradictory to the frame of the inquiry and would therein have displaced the awe of unknowing with a more certain perspective. To find means that would reflect the qualities of the data as well as holding it in ways which the students could interact with and draw from, I pulled on the experience of my playwork doctoral research (Guilbaud, 2011). Having through that work developed capacity and trust in the process of using the detail of the data to frame its presentation, I listened to the way that expressions in each participant's responses connected with other aspects, the way that respondents made connections and pointed to overlaps within what they were telling. I also noticed the way that details between recipients could fit into each other, offering different possible reflections and extensions of meaning – even where responses had been to the offered questions specifically they shed different light into other responses in a seemingly limitless possibility of configuration.

In this process of being moved by the data and working with it to create a frame I returned, for reassurance, to Richardson and St Pierre's (2005) description of refracted understanding. I was reminded of their proposition of an ever-evolving crystal as a more appropriate metaphor than a triangle for verification within modern qualitative research, and the recognition of the continuing impact of the data and process on the means of its appraisal (Guilbaud, 2011).

The flexibility of conjunction within each response and across them, interacted with my sensing within the responses of a tone of self-probing, of puzzling areas of uncertain awareness. These qualities materialised representationally into the creation of a giant puzzle. The puzzle pieces could be arranged and rearranged into any configuration. Each piece held a part of the responses from the playworkers in the field, offering the playwork students flexibility to play with meaning and association in myriad connections.

Communications of self – expressions, connections and resonances

An illustrative selection of extracts from the contributions of the playwork field, which were offered to the playwork students, hand written onto the puzzle pieces, is presented here.

In sharing these contributions within the structure of an article, there is necessarily a sacrifice of the flexible non-lineal quality that the puzzle pieces playfully offered as reflection of content and tone of what was expressed. As part of the opening up of connectivity and interpretation and reconfiguration of meaning, the words on the puzzle pieces were left anonymous. This enabled one contribution to flow into another's sentences and avoided the elevating of importance of certain offerings in relation to the perceived status of the contributor. However within this article format it was felt important to attribute the contributions.

In selecting the segments to present here, the attempt has been to offer a sense of the conversational resonances between what was expressed, to this end it was considered important to include discussion that illustrated subtlety and diversity of content rather than all that was offered. For example, in relation to experiences of playwork places – within the constraints of article length, it was only possible to present a fraction of the data here, with the additional omission of artistic contributions. Though editing of that which is included has been kept to a minimum, the very selection, and positioning of one paragraph after another, and within the loosely formed structuring subsections, creates an unavoidable lens of meaning making, a 'pointing to' which inescapably makes the presentation of data an act of analysis. It is hoped that the reader will play a little with the segments holding different combinations of paragraphs against each other, thus illuminating other meanings and probing their own resonances.

Stumbling accidentally home to playwork

Fraser Brown – I did fall into it … I was working as a student in New Merton Board Mills and the guys I was working with sent me off to get a sandwich and as I walked across the factory all the lights went out and I took two steps forward and went down a hole in the ground. As I went down I managed to grab something and pull myself back out and I was covered in wood pulp which is the most awful smell you can possibly imagine and I sat there in the dark cause you couldn't see a thing and when the lights came back on someone came across and looked at me and said what happened to you and I told him I just fell down that hole and he went and got a pole that must have been 20 feet long and put it down the hole on and on down the hole and he said 'look at that, that's where that goes'. So I could have fallen down that hole and disappeared and no one would have known where I'd gone or anything and I was so horrified. I walked out and I went and sat in Colliers Wood Rec, with a friend of mine and I was still covered in this shit, and we sat there and some bloke was running a playscheme – there were four or five people in tracksuits trying to run a playscheme, I think they may have even outnumbered the kids, and we sat there saying 'this is shit'; this is awful; we could do better than this, and because I had just fallen down that hole I said yeah I'm going to do this, I'm not going to do that stupid job anymore, mainly because I was so frightened so I jacked in that job and set about running a playscheme.

There was a whole gang of us, bloody arrogant students. One of my friends was a teacher and he knew his way round Colliers Wood, and we gave it two weeks to pull together this playscheme all along the lines of we could do it better than this council one which was being run in such a bad way and we just created this playscheme in the space of two weeks and we did all sorts of things that you could not do now, we built giant puppets and this is how we started the playscheme, we went all around the streets of Colliers Wood with these huge puppets doing a kind of Pied Piper thing just collecting children as we went all around. It took about an hour, with a band, I was playing guitar or something, and people were playing pipes, round Colliers Wood and into the park, where we had two people with the early days of the inflatable, and the guys said that when they started blowing this thing up it was as if children appeared from underneath it and before it was blown up even they were swamped with children and by the time we got to the park we must have had at least a hundred children in tow and we got all sorts of stuff in the park and we just had a good time with the kids

Clair Meares – How did I get into playwork … . I moved to Birmingham about twenty-five years ago and set up a whole host of interviews, and kind of walked into a community centre, a playwork situation, believing I was going for a completely different job in the bar or something like that, and ended up chatting about playwork, and actually I'd started out as a fine artist, which is a very common thing in playwork, a fine art background, or a creative background most definitely, and they happened to be looking for someone to compliment the team who had particular creative skills, although its creativity in a very different sense, and initially having come from the academic fine art background, it gave me some problems – I really had to get my head round that one very early on … the whole create and destroy element of it.

Wendy Russell – As a student I used to work in London, typing crossword clues for the daily newspapers which was a really good way of earning money but was boring as hell, and a friend from university who also lived in London said, come and be a playworker, so like so many people at the time in the 70 s I fell into playwork utterly by mistake, turned up terrified on my first day because I knew nothing about kids, I knew nothing about these kids lives, and I didn't know whether they would rip me to shreds.

And it was really interesting because I instantly felt at home, and I felt at home and among like-minded people with the other playworkers and I felt, this actually means something to me.

The biggest thing for me, and this is quite telling, was that sense of a community of practice, I never never felt isolated even in the worst moments, and at the same time there were certain things that you couldn't admit to in that community of practice

Simon Rix – I was brought up in West London amongst, though I didn't realise it at the time, a relatively radical milieu and a fairly radical era. I got a scholarship to a private school where I so did not fit in. My libertarianism and class-consciousness was nurtured by adversity, but I had no idea of how to pursue them. School and I willingly parted company, and I worked as a CSV in St Mungo's hostel for the homeless for a year. Here, I came across the solidarity and playfulness of street kid culture. My CSV came to an end, not least because of the amount of street kids who'd taken up residence in my room. We all had an 'F' in a circle tattooed, for 'family'.

Through my Gran, who was involved in local politics (as a Tory), I was introduced to Frank, a wealthy local socialist. He had started War on Want and Mencap, and his large house was turned over to his work with rooms filled with stuff for distribution and offices for the various organisations he worked in and with. My Gran may have been a Tory, but she knew a good human being when she saw one, and she recognised that Frank and I had stuff in common. He offered to try me out at this adventure playground he was involved with, and if we got on, then he would pay me volunteer expenses for a year from his trust. When I got to the adventure, I felt that I was home. The playworkers and other volunteers were all well left of centre and the ethos was definitely libertarian. This was a different kind of solidarity, but much akin to what I felt deriving with kids in the West End. I had previously felt so isolated, standing alone and yelling at the National Front as they marched down Hounslow High Street at the weekend and being taken away by cops – for my own safety. After that year was up, I went and did the Diploma in Playleadership at Thurrock, but I had to get an A level first, which a retired history teacher taught me over her kitchen table in nine months. I started the diploma just after having finally broken with living in the family home and moving in with one of my street kid family, who had a squat in Islington, a convenient place to be a trainee playworker, really, and to be an anarchist squatter. So that's where I went on to make my home. I never saw Frank again, but I will be grateful to him forever, and if I aspire to be anyone, it is to be him.

Bob Hughes – I'd just come from being a youth worker, I had a youth-work mentality … I came into playwork really to help children, so I came in as an interventionist as well. What was strange is that I went through a metamorphosis in the first couple of years I was there, and couldn't work out what my function was for at least that period of time, every time I looked at the kids, I thought that isn't what I need to be doing I need to be doing something else … And what came to pass was that, the site of the playground was on an old farmland on the outskirts of the town that I'd lived in and I'd played there as a child, that whole area had been a playground for me, the resonance of that and the resonance of the children playing on that spot again, began to make me realise, or at least I began to acknowledge that there was another function … and that's really where I got the title for that little red book, – 'notes for adventure playworkers', (see Hughes, 1975) it was only then that I began to realise that our primary function was not intervention but in making sure those kids were able to play. It's taken me ever since to try and work out what I meant.

Experiences of playwork identity

Clair Meares – One of the joyous things for me is reflecting on that element of serendipity and numerous other sort of things that *just happen in that way*, part of being a playworker is to be able to have that as an approach and to accept that and to be able to transmit that as an approach with the kids and the young people that you're working with.

Bob Hughes – I do see myself as a playworker and that's an identity I couldn't escape, it's been part of me for too long, and I think about applications and behaviour everywhere I go, not every second, but everywhere I go. I don't think there's a time when that switch is off, apart from if I'm asleep or ill. Almost all the time I'm open to suggestion, even if I'm not consciously thinking about play or playwork the door is open, so things gets logged in, it will just happen and then suddenly I'm doing it.

Wendy Russell – It is an outlook on life … even though it changes all the time.

I was a playworker before I was a parent, my experiences as a playworker informed how I was as a parent, my politics informed how I was as a parent and how I am as a grandparent and how I am still as a parent of a daughter who's a mother.

I'm a very political playworker. I was then and I am now, because these kids are always at the bottom of the heap. We have to recognise that adventure playgrounds, open access playwork, are funded in areas of deprivation. We're talking about working with very particular children in very particular circumstances. Of course playwork is important in other instances but it's not so desperately important that that's paid for out of the public purse.

Whereas adventure playgrounds in areas of deprivation, are part of a patchwork. They aren't the ones that are going to make everything alright, but they are part of a patchwork of children's daily lives and their family's daily lives that make things slightly better, slightly more manageable, particularly if they do things like feed them. It's the above and beyond commitment. Its part and parcel of being a part of those families' lives, those communities' lives.

Morgan Leichter-Saxby – I understand myself to be a playworker in my bones. It's more a vocation than a job for me, with a feeling of coming home because it speaks to so much that I'd long suspected was wrong, but not known how to address! Playwork challenges me, tests me, pushes me to become a better person. Playwork has taught me to practice and value patience, kindness, and what's happening in the moment. Those aren't messages I'd necessarily received from society at large.

Unknowingness is my default state when I'm with children directly. They're leading this exploration, even if I'm carrying some of the gear. I don't pretend to know what they're thinking or planning, or to assume that I'm still needed. It's a constant process for me to remember how little I know, to listen rather than prompt (because that training runs deep) but it's extended usefully throughout my academic work as well. And life!

Katherine Fisher (now Press) – From the very early stages of my son's life, it became obvious to me that I had to be very aware of his play cues. Trying to figure out what he was asking me to do or what he wanted to do for himself was all done through little play cues. I think now that I was getting some things right and some things wrong. I felt that I was always searching for the thing that would make him happy and contented. On the few occasions where I relaxed, slowed down and entered into what you could call a state of Negative Capability things started to happen and possibilities opened up. It was then that I realised that playwork was going to play a vital role in motherhood. Of course there were times where total exhaustion took over and I just wanted him to just tell me what he wanted but every time without fail if I slowed down and stopped trying to solve a situation quickly and in my own way, then it seemed to work.

When in playwork settings I have always tried very hard to look at the bigger picture of what is going on, I have always tried not to rush to try and solve a situation and have always put the children first. Since being a mother with the rush of the London life around me I know I have missed play cues and have sometimes really struggled with discipline. I know that children appreciate continuity and it is important to be consistent but I think I have sometimes felt some conflict between being a playworker and being a mum.

Maybe this will explain it a bit better: we were coming home from the Horniman Museum and gardens after a really lovely afternoon. We had been playing by some rose bushes, my son described the smell of the roses as the smell of love which I thought was lovely and very poetic! My daughter decided to pick some petals. On the way back my daughter held her petals and was asking me to sniff them, then she would break them up into little pieces and throw them away. We did this but I had to stop the buggy every time. Suddenly the weather changed from sunshine to showers and I decided that the game had to finish and had to get home as soon as possible – my daughter burst into tears! I told her we had to get home before it got wet. Then I realised that all we would be is wet, we lived just around the corner and would be home soon, my son loves puddles and my daughter was enjoying the petal game. So we started the game again, stopping and sniffing the petals and my son jumping in puddles beside me. What better thing could there be?

Awareness of merging of playwork selves and personal creativity

Wendy Russell – A huge number of playworkers have some kind of creative bent, whether that's arts … music. The number of playworkers who are musicians is phenomenal and I've always had this dream of getting them all together to play. And I think that's interesting in terms of divergent thinking in terms of wonder and unknowingness and those kinds of things.

But, you have to have a repertoire of responses, you have to practice.

People talk about improvisation as an approach to working with kids and think that it means making things up on the spot and its far from that, you'd be no good as a Jazz improvisational musician if you didn't practice 8 hours a day learn your scales, know the rules and then know how to bend them. There's technical skill involved as well as creativity

Simon Rix – Probably, yes (there is overlap), but as playwork is where I developed as a person from the age of 17, I can't really unentangle them. I'm not an 'artist' (and I certainly would never practice artism) nor am I a writer, builder, or musician, but all of these things have come into my playwork and been developed through it. I am a bit of a cook – we used to run squat cafes back in the day, and I use that in playwork a lot.

Kelda Lyons – I explore the city and nature. I like not knowing and being lost, other people call it lost, I call it fun!

Joel Seath – If I think carefully there are many crossovers between my writing-form-ongoing-experiment and my view of play (by which I mean, not just what I think of play but how I see it in the moment) – These crossovers are the moment about the moment, the precision and the possible (even in the apparent chaos), the rhythm and the grace, the seen and the in-between, in looks and sightedness, in 'just-known-unsaidness'.

Bob Hughes – I don't think its random, because its within parameters that I couldn't help but set because I've been doing this for 40 odd years, my whole being is this work. It's all I think about really, so the process starts of its own volition and does what it does, it kicks off and I'll be in a daze for a period of time, and if it's formulated enough to be put into words I might write it in a notebook and it will either or not feed into some other thinking later on, I think in pictures, it's very fast, I dip into a memory and then come out because they've confirmed what I was thinking about What do they look like?

The places I know, like a storyboard almost, people I know, places I know, I can imagine, so a lot of this is not about places I know at all, I dream a lot, and they have a place to play, and they have a very important place to play, but an awful lot of my – I'll dignify it by calling it thinking, but its different to that – the process that I find myself going through; it's uncontrolled; it's the construction of an idea from endless sources; it's almost like the picture; it is a coming together of things, that create the picture, and they're being drawn from all over the place; they're being drawn from experiences yesterday and memories 40 years ago; they're being drawn from how somebody said something. I can still remember children on the first playground I worked on, how they addressed one another and how they spoke. I can remember snapshots, and it's important.

Relationships with the playground

Fraser Brown – I spent most evenings up in the area talking to the kids, and we kind of created the idea that this place is going to be your place. We used to go round marking out with little sticks where the fence was going to be and we must have done that a dozen times, and it never occurred to me that the kids were taking the sticks away in the day, just so they could do it again, you know it's good fun, working out where your fence is going to go …

When they started building the playground building it was a site hut and they told the kids that in order to erect this site hut you had to have a level slab of concrete and the builders told the kids that if anything happened to that slab of concrete while it was setting they wouldn't be able to erect the site hut and that it needed two weeks to settle, and a group of kids camped out every night protecting their slab of concrete.

Simon Rix – There's one guy, who comes regularly with stuff and he put us on to the company trust which donated some money. There was a presentation last week where several bigwigs came along to have their pictures taken. He said to them all, 'What I like about this place is that every time I come there's something different, something has changed.' He was looking at some round table tops he'd brought us which we'd mounted dining chairs between so that they were crazy rocking chairs. They're not actually all that popular to play in for long, but they look off the wall and so contribute to the permissional and out of the ordinary ambience we attempt to construct.

Joel Seath – The permissional thing is important, I think: not only with access to stuff but also with the whole swearing debate and other ways of being.

With our children, I think, there's a general acceptance of how things are with the working-ness/not workingness. I put a rickety old table up on a pallet jetty type construction the other day because I couldn't lower the rope swing for the child in question to access easier. She tried it, got on with it, we got rid of the table because it ricketed! She swung in other ways.

I see the loop, in a way, on the playground lately ... I am object ... the children play me, reconstitute me, re-layer the previous narratives, they also seem to know how to suspect reality and wait for me to come back ...

Wendy Russell – In an Adventure Playground it is easier for the space to be open, and open to not knowing, and open to uncertainty, and open to all those types of things that characterise children's play, simply because it is a dedicated space that has its own culture, that doesn't get colonised by others. Newer playworkers come to build that repertoire of responses alongside other more experienced ones. However they can pick up the habits that close down space as well as feeling comfortable with the uncertainty

Clair Meares – My understanding of Negative Capability is the feeling that you need to work outside and consciously act against some of the dominant paradigms that we have around children and young people and in situations that we find ourselves, which are very varied and most usually not ideal playwork situations, we need to find ways of consciously working outside those.

At one site which was far less than what I might think of as an ideal playwork situation, the playworkers were consciously using the space and subverting what might be normative expectations as to how they would behave in particular parts of the setting or in particular situations. They were just having to work that much harder but it was with a consciousness that they worked harder ... .Had they come in and been completely new workers (and again this was evident with the new workers that were there, the new workers were falling into a kind of supervisory, a very distant supervisory mode, of being with the children and the young people), the experienced long term workers who had experience outside of that setting or before the way that it had been re-arranged after they'd had a big lottery input, it was those workers who were kind of consciously doing this Negative Capability.

In closing – responding to uncertainty, a catalyst towards the questioning of self as playworker

To offer today's university students the experience of a class without learning outcomes, without specified requirement, without assessment or defined application, is already to introduce a certain bewilderment. To take an inexpert position – inexpert in reflection of the playworker's presence within the play space, as expressed in discrete lived experience by the playworkers in the field – to share my personal sense of awe at the degree of self-revelation in those contributions, and to invite the students to find their own meanings and connections between, and in relation to the content of the puzzle pieces, caused discernible confusion for some.

The de-structuring of this time at the beginning of the students' preparation for their experiential learning programme was a deliberate attempt to destabilise the static of playwork as a book-bound abstract, and to value the integrity within playwork identity, of the experiences of uncertainty and self-questioning that practice generates.

Within their interactions with the puzzles pieces the students were encouraged to create responsively and add their own pieces. They were offered the possibility of incorporating content and response into the beginnings of a self-created notebook for reflective questioning and musings within the upcoming months of their experiential playwork practice.

The tentative nature of their own contributions to the puzzle, was atmospherically palpable yet there was also a feeling of relaxing into the permissional sense of the situation, enabled by the session structure and the offerings from the field as they explored these; laughter, playfulness, and irreverence held the space for engagement with uncertainty. Their words were self-questioning and probing, bravely revealing their own reflexive uncertainty with their capacity for playwork – though less detailed, their expressions were nonetheless in tune with this ever present aspect within the contributions from the field. Their own explorations touched on awareness of relationship to playwork as a calling and as a choice, for some a choice still unsettled. There was questioning of what playwork is, and of its value; and a wondering of what might be hoped for in the political realm.

From the position of researcher, of inquiry and evaluation it would have been gratifying to come back together with this group, either at the end of their preparation for practice programme or at the end of their experiential playwork placements. It would have been interesting to explore further layers of their sense of playwork identity together and to facilitate further interactions with the depth and volume of contributions from the field.

However, there is also an awareness that such a revisiting might have come with a degree of expectation, a reflection on the value of this work in relation to perceived development in the students' relationship to their sense of playwork identity and to the contributions from the field. Such a situation would have been counter to the impetus of the project and may have contradicted its framing within the qualities of uncertainty and unknowingness inherent to playwork. Rather it seems appropriate that the students were offered a catalyst with the possibility of re-engaging with the content of the puzzle pieces online and the invitation to contact the contributors from the field for further discussion as they wished. Furthermore it is anticipated that these and other possibilities for interaction will become available to future playwork students, enabling the extension of a resource of stimulus and reflection belonging evermore to the student body.

There is, perhaps in the similar evaluative vein, the temptation to conclude this article with a validating flourish, contextualised with comparative and theoretical reference. However, the considerations discussed in opening remain as pertinent in closing. The potential ripples of this project are far from quantifiable, or even qualitatively foreseeable. In remaining authentic to the nature of this endeavour it is simply hoped that all those who took part, both playworkers in the field and playwork students will have in some way, either at the time or in some future conjunction of memory and moment gained perspective towards themselves within their playwork. It is also hoped the reader will be moved in their own way to perpetuate a sensitivity towards the playing child through the valuing of their own experiences of wonder, humility and particular sense of negative capability.

Disclosure statement

No potential conflict of interest was reported by the author

Note

1. For example Fisher contextualized awareness gained through her practice in relation to Keats' Negative Capability: Fisher (2008) Playwork in the early years: working in a parallel profession. In: Brown, F. & Taylor, C. (eds.) *Foundations of playwork*. Maidenhead, Open University Press. pp. 174–178.

   Else and Sturrock integrated and adapted ideas from Gregory Bateson, Erving Goffman, C.G. Jung and D.W. Winnicott, in the forming of their proposition of *psycholudics* which was to become a fundamental frame of reference for playwork: Sturrock and Else (1998) The playground as therapeutic space playwork as healing *IPA/USA Triennial National Conference, Play in a Changing Society Research,*

Design, Application. June 1998, Colorado USA.

Meares drew on Polanyi's notion of the tacit dimension of knowledge and Deleuze's concept of 'rhizome' in creating a research framework that was responsive to her playwork practice: Meares (2015) *Making the tacit* 'good enough' – *exploring the tacit dimension in the relationship between play-worker and playing child.* Masters in Youth and Community Development, University of Birmingham.

References

Brown, F. (1989). *Working with children: A playwork training pack.* Leeds: Children First.

Brown, F. (2003). Compound flexibility: The role of playwork in child development. In F. Brown (Ed.), *Playwork theory and practice* (pp. 51–65) Buckingham: Open University Press.

Brown, F. (2008). The fundamentals of playwork. In F. Brown & C. Taylor (Eds.), *Foundations of playwork* (pp. 7–13). Maidenhead: Open University Press.

Brown, F. (2014). *Play and playwork, 101 stories of children playing.* Maidenhead: Open University Press.

Davy, A. (2007). Playwork: Art, science, political movement of religion. In W. Russell, B. Hanscomb, & J. Fitzpatrick, (Eds.), *Playwork voices* (pp. 41–46). London: The London Centre for Playwork Education and Training.

Davy, A., & Gallagher, J. (2006). *New playwork.* London: Thomson.

Else, P. (2008). Playing: The space between. In F. Brown & C. Taylor (Eds.), *Foundations of playwork* (pp. 79–83). Maidenhead: Open University Press.

Erikson, E. H. (1963). *Childhood and society.* New York: W.W. Norton.

Erikson, E. H. (1980). *Identity and the life cycle, volume 1.* New York: W.W. Norton.

Farrow, T., Stevens, V., & Stanley, S. (2003). *Playwork candidate handbook, NVQ/SVQ and CACHE level 2.* Oxford: Heinemann.

Fisher, K. (2008). Playwork in the early years: Working in a parallel profession. In F. Brown & C. Taylor (Eds.), *Foundations of playwork* (pp. 174–178). Maidenhead: Open University Press.

Guilbaud, S. (2011). A phenomenological inquiry into the possibility of played-with-ness in experiences with things. Doctor of Philosophy: Leeds Metropolitan University.

Guilbaud, Vignoles. (2014). *An invitation to participate in research around playwork identity, playfulness, creativity and negative capability.* Eastbourne: Play and Playwork Lmt. iP-D!P Magazine, Issue 228, November 14, p. 19.

Hanscomb, B., & Virdi, M. (2007). Playwork learning – sharing the journey. In W. Russell, B. Hanscomb, & J. Fitzpatrick (Eds.), *Playwork voices* (pp. 176–185). London: The London Centre for Playwork Education and Training.

Henricks, T. (2015). *Play and the human condition.* Urbana: University of Illinois Press.

Hughes, B. (1975). *Notes for adventure playworkers.* London: Childs Play.

Hughes, B. (1996a). *Play environments a question of quality.* London: PLAYLINK.

Hughes, B. (1996b). *A playworker's taxonomy of playtypes.* London: PLAYLINK.

Hughes, B. (2001). *Evolutionary playwork and reflective analytic practice.* London: Routledge.

Hughes, B. (2006). *Play types, speculations and possibilities.* London: London Centre for Playwork Education and Training.

Keats, J. (1817). *Letters to George and Tom.* Retrieved from http://www.mrbauld.com/negcap.html.

Kilvington, J., & Wood, A. (2010). *Reflective playwork.* London: Continuum.

Kroger, J., & Marcia, J. E. (2011). The identity statuses: Origins, meanings, and interpretations. In S. J. Schwartz, K. Luyckx, & V. L. Vignoles (Eds.), *Handbook of identity theory and research* (pp. 31–54). New York: Springer.

Meares, C. (2015). *Making the tacit 'good enough' – exploring the tacit dimension in the relationship between playworker and playing child*. Masters in Youth and Community Development: University of Birmingham, UK.

Melville, S. (2007). From intuition to understanding. In W. Russell, B. Hanscomb, & J. Fitzpatrick (Eds.), *Playwork voices* (pp. 4–9). London: The London Centre for Playwork Education and Training.

Newstead, S. (2004). *The buskers guide to playwork*. Eastleigh: Common Threads.

Richardson, L., & St. Pierre, E. A. (2005). Writing: A method of inquiry. In N. K. Denzin & Y. S. Lincoln (Eds.), *The Sage handbook of qualitative research* (3th ed. pp. 959–978). London: Sage.

Russell, W., Hanscomb, B., & Fitzpatrick, J. (Eds.). (2007). *Playwork voices*. London: The London Centre for Playwork Education and Training.

Schwartz, S. J., Luyckx, K., & Vignoles, V. L. (2011). Introduction: Towards an integrated view of identity. In S. J. Schwartz, K. Luyckx & V. L. Vignoles, (Eds.), *Handbook of identity theory and research* (pp. 1–27). New York: Springer.

Seath, J. (2013). Heretical speculations about some children's play wishes: From adulteration to a fusion of play *Playworkings* [Internet blog]. Retrieved May 20, 2015, from https://playworkings.wordpress.com/2013/06/07/heretical-speculation-about-some-childrens-play-wishes-from-adulteration-to-a-fusion-of-play/

Seath, J. (2015). Underneath our stories of play *Playworkings* [Internet blog]. Retrieved May 5, 2015, from https://playworkings.wordpress.com/2015/05/04/underneath-our-stories-of-play/

Spariosu, M. (1989). *Dionysus reborn: Play and the aesthetic dimension in modern philosophical and scientific discourse*. New York: Cornell University Press.

Spariosu, M. (2013). Exile and utopia as liminal play: A cultural-theoretical approach. *Philosophy at Play*. April 9–10, University of Gloucestershire. p. 13.

Sturrock, G., & Else, P. (1998). *The playground as therapeutic space: playwork as healing. IPA/USA Triennial National Conference, Play in a Changing Society: Research, Design, Application. June 1998*. Retrieved September 25, 2015, from www.ludemos.co.uk.

Taylor, C. (2008). Some reflections on the history of playwork in the adventure playground tradition. In F. Brown & C. Taylor (Eds.), *Foundations of playwork* (pp. 128–131). Maidenhead: Open University Press.

Weber, M., Owen, D. S., Strong, T. B., & Livingstone, R. (2004). *The vocation lectures*. Indianapolis: Hackett Publishing Company.

Wetherell, M. (2010). The field of identity studies. In M. Wetherell & C. T. Mohanty (Eds.), *The SAGE handbook of identities* (pp. 3–26). London: Sage.

Ethical practice for the playwork practitioner

David Stonehouse

This paper discusses the importance of ethics for play and playwork practitioners as the sector and work force move towards becoming a recognised profession within the United Kingdom. Exactly what is meant by the term ethics is defined, before moving on to a discussion of two key areas. First, the ethical framework known as F.A.I.R. (this mnemonic stands for Fairness, respect for Autonomy, Integrity, and to seek the most beneficial and least harmful consequences or Results) devised by Rowson [2006. *Working ethics: How to be fair in a culturally complex world*. London: Jessica Kingsley) and second, the four ethical principles of Beauchamp and Childress (2013. *Principles of biomedical ethics* (7th ed.). Oxford: Oxford University Press]. Throughout links are made to the eight Playwork Principles developed by the Playwork Principles Scrutiny Group, Cardiff in 2005 and endorsed by SkillsActive (2013a. *Playwork principles* [Internet]. Retrieved August 26, 2015, from http://www.skillsactive.com/PDF/ sectors/Playwork_Principles.pdf).

Introduction

Playwork is becoming more and more professional and rightly so. Now with the development of the Playwork Register (SkillsActive, 2013b) and with minimum levels of qualifications being required for registration, the question of ethics and how they apply to playwork will become more and more important. The eight Playwork Principles are stated as being 'the professional and ethical framework for playwork' (SkillsActive, 2013a). They list eight statements which embody the role and beliefs which playwork practitioners and anyone working with children and young people should have in regard to playwork. However, do playwork practitioners understand what this truly means? Do practitioners recognise how these eight statements can be applied professionally and ethically in their own practice? And importantly, how will playwork practitioners know that they are acting in an ethical playwork way for their children, young people, families, colleagues and the wider communities that they live and work within?

Often when ethical decisions present themselves the issues involved are complex and the way ahead is not always clear. Opposing viewpoints and differences of opinion need to be considered carefully before choosing the right course of action. The aim of this article is, therefore, to examine and explore what is meant by the term ethics and importantly how this can be applied to everyday playwork practice. Two key ethical frameworks, Rowson's (2006) F.A.I.R. and

Beauchamp and Childress's (2013) four ethical principles, will be discussed and linked to the Playwork Principles (SkillsActive, 2013a).

What is ethics?

First of all, it is important to define exactly what is meant by the term ethics. Thinking in an ethical way is about striving to do the right thing. It is about making the right choice for the individual playwork practitioner, but more importantly for the children and young people they are working with and for. Hugman (2005, p. 160) states that 'the purpose of ethics is to pose questions that challenge thought and action'. Therefore, playwork practitioners through thinking in an ethical way should challenge themselves to consider how they act and think in all situations. Berglund (2007) goes further to state that ethics is a process of reflection. Through reflecting upon their actions, playwork practitioners should challenge how they think and what they do. As Stonehouse (2011a) states, reflection is about examining practice and why actions and decisions were chosen.

Thinking in an ethical way also allows the playwork practitioner to examine their 'life as members of a community, and how we behave and function within society' (Thompson, Melia, Boyd, & Horsburgh, 2006, p. 36). As a playwork practitioner, how does our everyday practice impact upon the community and importantly the wider society that we live and work within? How does society and our immediate environment impact upon our role as a playwork practitioner? Do we promote children's rights to play and always act in the best interests of the play users within our community? Are we vocal champions for play? As stated in Playwork Principle No. 1 (SkillsActive, 2013a), play 'is fundamental to the healthy development and well-being of individuals and communities'. Considering playwork practice in an ethical way and recognising that membership of the local and wider community is important in terms of play, will assist the playwork practitioner to be an invaluable resource and advocate for children and young people as well as the communities they live and work within.

Being ethical is not just about reducing our carbon footprint by sourcing our break time snacks from a local supplier. It is not about making sure that the playwork setting always recycles or saves energy. It is not about how the setting impacts upon its immediate neighbours, being considerate to others needs, for example, in regard to excessive noise pollution. It is not about considering the impact the setting may have on those service users coming through the doors, for example, is the food provided always healthy or with a vegetarian option. Are the dietary requirements of all children and young people met and welcomed? Being ethical is not even about the playwork practitioner being a happy, enthusiastic, positive thinking, forward thinking and passionate about play person all of the time. Though all of these former things are good responsible work place practices, and the latter a good personal and professional mindset, though unrealistic for most normal human beings to behave like this consistently, ethical practice goes much deeper than all these.

Often in the reader's daily lives as well as within playwork practice, choices will have to be made. Sometimes the right decision is obvious and clear cut and there are no alternative viewpoints to consider (Stonehouse, 2012). There is clearly a right and a wrong choice. However, we can often be faced with a dilemma where the right choice is not always clear and where differences of opinion may seem equally valid (Thompson et al., 2006). How does the playwork practitioner attempt to please everybody all of the time? When inevitably this is not possible, how is the best course of action decided upon?

Policies, procedures and even the Playwork Principles (SkillsActive, 2013a) do not always inform the playwork practitioner exactly what to do in every situation. As Rowson (2006, pp. 121–122) states, 'professionals must constantly make autonomous judgements since even when there are professional rules of thumb or guidelines from advisory committees relevant to their situation they may have to decide how to relate them to their particular circumstances'. How a decision is decided upon is often down to the individual playwork practitioner's own ethical viewpoint – what is believed is correct and fair and just at that moment in time while adhering to policy. Ethical practice is about deciding on the right way forward, making the right decisions within a set of circumstances, after careful consideration of all the foreseeable potential outcomes and consequences. Of course, the difficulty is that not every outcome is foreseeable and even good intentions and plans do not always turn out right. However, having utilised ethical thinking in the decision-making process and having considered seriously all probable and potential outcomes, the decision that is finally arrived at should be the best course of action at that time, given the situation and the information to hand.

Of course, we have all been, and continue to be, affected over time by a large range of influences which help to develop and mould and create our own personal ethical viewpoint. Unless we consciously sit down and consider what these influences may be, they largely go unnoticed and affect us without our knowledge. All life experiences which we have, both good and bad, will have an effect upon how we think, feel and act. They make us the special, unique person that we are. No two people will experience things throughout their lives, in exactly the same way. An individual's beliefs, their upbringing and family influences, their circle of friends, a person's religious education and beliefs, together with their spirituality (and equally as important if a person practises no religion), all assist in the decision-making process. The education and training we have received whether it is playwork based or not will influence how we practice and think. Role models within our workplace will positively influence us and challenge and inspire us to a higher level of practice. Experts and respected authors within the field of playwork and other disciplines, together with the Playwork Principles and playwork organisations all shape and inform our professional practice.

No two people, let alone two playwork practitioners, will have exactly the same ethical beliefs. Hopefully there are a few things which the majority will all hold to be true. On the face of it, it can be stated that everyone accepts and believes that murder is wrong, however some people do commit. If we then bring in discussions around capital punishment and the rightness or wrongness of war, then it starts to become even more unclear. Differences of opinion and debate will ensue. To aid practitioners working within the UK there are the eight Playwork Principles (SkillsActive, 2013a) which hopefully everyone working within the field of playwork can embrace. However, because play occurs in many different settings and environments and is facilitated by a wide range of different individuals from different professional backgrounds, it is possible and even highly likely that not everyone will be able to accept or even know or agree with part or all of them. The most recent SkillsActive (2015) strategy document reported that employers say that there is a gap between the level of skill that they need to run their business and the level of skill that they currently have in their workforce.

The first Playwork Principle (SkillsActive, 2013a) states that 'All children and young people need to play. The impulse to play is innate. Play is a biological, psychological and social necessity, and is fundamental to the healthy development and well-being of individuals and communities.' This first principle clearly states the importance of play to both the individual child and society as a whole. As Hughes (2012, p. 66) states, it is a 'strong affirmation both of the source of play and its importance to physical and mental health'. Therefore, from the outset the focus of the playwork practitioner's role should be to assist and facilitate children and young people to play.

The third Playwork Principle (SkillsActive, 2013a) states that 'The prime focus and essence of playwork is to support and facilitate the play process and this should inform the development of play policy, strategy, training and education.' Everything a playwork practitioner does should have at its centre play. Play comes first, not secondary to other issues.

Therefore to aid playwork practice, professional and ethical frameworks such as Rowson's (2006) F.A.I.R. and Beauchamp and Childress's (2013) ethical principles, together with the eight Playwork Principles (SkillsActive, 2013a), can help playwork practitioners to have a common ground on which to base their ethical decision making. A good playwork practitioner, delivering and facilitating quality play opportunities, should be working within and be guided by these ethical principles and frameworks, using them as a basis for their decision-making.

Rowson's (2006) ethical framework F.A.I.R.

Rowson (2006) developed the ethical framework known as F.A.I.R. to assist professionals working across all sectors of society. This mnemonic stands for Fairness, respect for Autonomy, Integrity, and to seek the most beneficial and least harmful consequences or Results. The first part of the framework, fairness, is about providing benefits to all equally, be that health care, education, welfare rights or even play. Can the playwork practitioner truthfully say that the play provision provided is open to all equally, that no child or young person is excluded, either knowingly or as a result of some thoughtless actions? Plowden (2010, p. 16) states 'disabled children, or those with specific needs, often miss out on the opportunity to play freely in an environment where they feel safe to do so'. In the fourth UK's report to the Committee on the Rights of the Child, the UK's Children's Commissioners reported that for disabled children 'fully inclusive play provision has yet to become a reality. In some cases, disabled children are provided with separate and discrete provision that is not freely chosen and leads to them being away from their peers' (Aynsley-Green, Marshall, Lewsley, & Towler, 2008, p. 29).

More recently, the KIDS (2013) Playday survey, completed by 952 respondents, reported that only 47% of people who work with children and young people stated that local services and play-spaces were accessible to disabled children and young people. Twenty-five per cent stated that local services and playspaces were not accessible, with a further 28% giving no response. Therefore, a quarter of all provisions considered in the survey in 2013, does not allow disabled children and young people to access play opportunities and facilities. Playwork Principle No. 5 (SkillsActive, 2013a) states that 'the role of the playworker is to support all children and young people in the creation of a space in which they can play'. As playwork practitioners it is our responsibility, both legally and ethically, to ensure that our play service allows all children to freely play within a safe and secure environment. On reflection can the playwork practitioner truthfully assert that all parts of their play service are truly inclusive? Are there activities where disabled children and young people are prevented from accessing? If this is so, then that is clearly not achieving the first part of Rowson's (2006) framework of being treated fairly. It is also not meeting Article 23 of the Convention on the Rights of the Child (UNICEF, 1991) which states that disabled children should be active participants in their community.

Rowson (2006) also focuses on the staff team, discussing that the allocation of responsibilities should be done fairly as well. Taking into account people's individual abilities, skills and preferences, these responsibilities should be shared out equally among all team members involved. However, do certain members of staff or volunteers within the play setting take on more responsibilities than other members of the team, simply because they are more willing or conscientious? Are there equally staff who avoid responsibilities for an easier time? As the person in charge or senior playwork practitioner within a setting it is our responsibility to recognise this unfairness and share responsibilities out equally. As the manager with staff training and development responsibilities (Stonehouse, 2013), are opportunities for training courses, conference attendance and further education allocated on a fair basis?

The second part of the framework is respect for autonomy. Rowson (2006, p. 53) states that professionals should 'respect people's autonomy as far as possible within a society in which the legitimate interests of all must be considered'. Griffith and Tengnah (2010, p. 29) define autonomy as meaning 'Self-rule with no control, undue influence or interference from others.' Rowson (2006) states that professionals should allow individuals to be in control of decisions about themselves, what they do, what is done to them, and have control over what happens to information about them. As playwork practitioners we need to enable children and young people to be in control of their play, allowing and enabling them to have a voice and to be heard. This links closely with Playwork Principle No. 2 (SkillsActive, 2013a). Play is freely chosen by the child or young person. It is directed by them, for their own reasons. Playwork practitioners should not interfere with this choice, or try to influence it in any way. The playworker's actions should be to facilitate this free choice and enable it to be realised. Within autonomy, if there is an outcome to the play, then it is whatever has been chosen by the player, and not by the adult. Equally valid is that the play has no outcome, or the outcome is unknown and not considered at the outset. It is play for play's sake. Of course this is all within safe boundaries, and as Rowson (2006) stated the legitimate interests of all must be considered within this.

The third part to the framework is integrity. Rowson (2006, p. 53) states that the professional needs 'to behave with integrity by acting in accord with the stated or implied values, undertakings and objectives of the profession'. This simply means that our actions and personal values should match our professional values. As playwork practitioners do we truly believe in and adhere to the Playwork Principles as guiding our everyday practice. If there is a conflict here then we need to recognise this and act professionally in line with the Playwork Principles and not with our own personal beliefs. If our personal beliefs and values do not match our professional ones then it is time to ask if the playwork practitioner is actually in the right profession. Integrity is about following through with what we believe to be right, both professionally and personally and this can only be achieved if these two beliefs are in harmony.

There is a close connection between integrity and fidelity. Fidelity concerns the relationship that exists between two people, principally the playwork practitioner and the child/young person. Edwards (2009) discusses the fidelity rule as being the commitment between one individual and another. It is about the playwork practitioner being faithful, always striving to keep promises, being trustworthy, showing respect and dignity, and always acting in the other person's best interest (Stonehouse, 2012). Playwork practitioners can demonstrate fidelity through always striving to follow the Playwork Principles, always delivering quality play opportunities to the best of their abilities, and knowing and working within the laws, guidelines and policies that govern their practice.

The last part of the framework is seeking the most beneficial and least harmful consequences, or results, for the individual and society (Rowson, 2006). There are two clear aims for the playwork practitioner. First, to produce as many benefits as possible and second, to avoid causing, and preventing any harm or negative outcomes as much as possible. As playwork practitioners it is important that risk assessments are performed correctly and not merely as an exercise in ticking the boxes. Think through all proposed actions as far as possible so that benefits are identified and increased and possible harmful consequences are removed.

Beauchamp and Childress's (2013) ethical principles

Moving on from Rowson's (2006) framework, Beauchamp and Childress (2013) have also developed four ethical principles which can aid professional practice. These are respect for autonomy, beneficence, non-maleficence and justice. The first principle, respect for autonomy is the same as that of Rowson's (2006). However, Beauchamp and Childress (2013) describe it as respecting other people's wishes and then supporting them in carrying out those wishes. We may not always be in agreement with the choices that others make, however we need to support their wishes, if it is safe to do so. Within playwork this means allowing the children to have complete control over their play environment and giving them free choice wherever this is possible. Playwork Principle No. 2 (SkillsActive, 2013a) states that 'Children and young people determine and control the content and intent of their play, by following their own instincts, ideas and interests, in their own way for their own reasons.' This is autonomy in action. It is the role then of the playwork practitioner to support children and young people in being able to do this. However, adults working with and alongside children and young people, in whatever field and environment, need to make sure that the play that is being facilitated is truly child led. When adults interfere with and become involved 'adulteration' of the playspace can occur (Wragg, 2008). As Sturrock and Else (1998, p. 20) state:

> there is a danger that the play aims and objects of the children become contaminated by, either the wishes of the adult in an urge to 'teach' or 'educate', simply to dominate, or by the worker's own unplayed out material.

This is something that needs to be closely guarded against. When this happens the child is no longer determining or controlling their own play but has become subservient to the wishes of the adult.

Loss of autonomy and free choice can also occur when play is designed to meet specific outcomes. The outcomes have been chosen by the adult, not the child, and may well be hidden and not communicated to the child. This can then change the activity from one which was play to one which is now task and possibly work like. The child is no longer participating in the play for their own reasons, but the reasons of the adult. Through this the child's autonomy is reduced and their freedom of choice is taken away.

The second ethical principle is that of beneficence. Berglund (2007, p. 12) defines this as 'the principle of doing good and providing care to others'. Edwards (2009) takes this further by describing it as the promotion of well-being. As playwork practitioners we need to be focusing our practice on always striving to do good while promoting the well-being of those children we are working for and with. This cannot always be taken for granted as, from time to time, we all bring negative issues and stress from our personal lives with us into our professional roles. As Playwork Principle No. 7 (SkillsActive, 2013a) states, playwork practitioners need to recognise the two-way impact that occurs between the adult and the playing child. Playwork practitioners need to make sure that the impact they are having is a positive one, thereby only doing good. They need to guard against bringing their own agendas albeit subconsciously to the play environment.

Playwork Principle No. 6 (SkillsActive, 2013a) highlights the importance of playwork practitioners having a sound knowledge and understanding of play and of being reflective in their practice. Having playwork practitioners who are well trained and experienced in delivering play opportunities will help to achieve this principle and to do good. As playwork practitioners, the questions need to be asked Are policies and procedures always followed? What is accepted to be best practice? Is the latest research acknowledged and taken on board? Is the playwork practitioner properly trained and fully competent to facilitate the play they are providing? Is it always of the highest possible standard and quality? If not, then everyone has both a professional duty and an ethical one to acknowledge this and to act upon it.

Playwork Principle No. 6 (SkillsActive, 2013a) asks the playwork practitioner to reflect upon their practice. Being a reflective playwork practitioner means that experiences are reviewed, through evaluation and analysis, so that lessons can be learnt (Johns, 2009). Reflection is not an activity to be done only when something has gone wrong, but should become the routine normal everyday activity of the playwork practitioner. Strengths and weaknesses, positives and negatives can be identified, and through this playwork practice can be evaluated and improved upon (Cottrell, 2008). Through reflective practice, the playwork practitioner can ensure that the ethical principle of doing good can be achieved, both in the immediate here and now, and for the future. By reflecting upon their own practice and then sharing these observations with their playwork colleagues, good and even exemplary practice can be identified and then cascaded to a wider audience, thereby benefitting all (Banks & Gallagher, 2009).

The third ethical principle is non-maleficence. Beauchamp and Childress (2013, p. 150) state that this is the obligation 'to abstain from causing harm to others'. It goes hand in hand with the previous one, beneficence, to do good. As Playwork Principle No. 8 (SkillsActive, 2013a) highlights, playwork practitioners 'must balance risk with the developmental benefit and well-being of children'. We may sometimes deny a child's free choice to prevent harm. This is where our risk assessments come in, which have to be fair and proportional, where our intervention style needs to enable play to be extended within safe but challenging boundaries. As Brussoni, Olsen, Pike, and Sleet (2012, p. 3134) state, there needs to be a move away from children being 'as safe as possible' to one of 'as safe as necessary'. Through doing this we will be facilitating children and young people to be able to extend their own play and not be constrained unnecessarily by over protective policies and procedures.

The last ethical principle of Beauchamp and Childress (2013) is justice. Justice is closely linked to Rowson's (2006) concept of fairness. Justice is simply defined by Hendrick (2004, p. 7) as 'equal treatment of equal cases'. This is about treating everyone the same. However, do all children within the playwork setting receive equal treatment? At first glance the playwork practitioner may categorically state yes they do, but look closer, do certain children demand more attention because they are more confident than some of their peers? Do those that are the loudest get heard first? Justice then is about recognising that some children within the setting may not be having an equal say in decisions, or equal chance at opportunities that should be open to all. Justice for the playwork practitioner then is about being aware of what is going on around them within the environment and being observant and sensitive to the needs of all children and young people.

An equally important issue within justice is we also need to recognise that some children and young people, as well as adults, will require special care and attention over and above what others may need (UNICEF, 1991). This is not about disadvantaging those not receiving extra care and attention, but it is rather 'about meeting everyone's individual needs fairly' (Stonehouse, 2012, p. 250). Giving extra care and attention to some, rather than others who do not require that extra care, is ethical as the playwork practitioner is treating everyone as an individual with individual needs which all need to be met.

Advocacy

Playwork principle No. 4 (SkillsActive, 2013a) states that 'playworkers act as advocates for play when engaging with adult led agendas'. Pithouse and Crowley (2007) describe advocacy as promoting the overall welfare of children while also challenging injustices. They go on to state that it is about any cooperative or individual action which aims to enrich the lives of children (Pithouse & Crowley, 2007); while Bracknell Forest Council (2012, p. 1) define advocacy as simply 'speaking up for, or acting on behalf of, yourself or another person'. Playwork practitioners, therefore, need to be advocates for the children and young people they come into contact with, so that they are truly equal partners within adult agendas. As Cole-Hamilton (2008) states, playwork practitioners need to make children active members together in the decision-making process. This is no easy task but one which all playwork practitioners need to strive for. As Davy and Gallagher (2006) state, it is the playwork practitioner who needs to ensure that children and young people's voices are heard and they are consulted on all aspects of the play provision they are using. It is about allowing and enabling the child's voice to be heard, and once heard that it is acted upon. Playwork practitioners also have to be aware of any barriers that are put up by adults to hinder this free expression and right of consultation. Lundy (2007) identified that adults often believe that children lack the necessary capacity to make a valuable contribution, or that giving children more say in decision-making will undermine adult authority or that consultation with children means too much time is taken. It is the playwork practitioner's responsibility to take down and challenge these barriers. As Article 12 of the UN Convention on the Rights of the Child states, the child who is capable of forming his or her own views should have 'the right to express those views freely in all matters affecting the child, the views being given due weight in accordance with the age and maturity of the child' (UNICEF, 1991).

Importantly being an advocate is also about making sure that children and young people are aware of their rights. This is both within play and within the wider society in which they live. They also need to understand how to access those rights fully. As an adult, is the playwork practitioner fully aware of all the rights that they personally have? How less informed might children be? It is important therefore that playwork practitioners become experts in children's rights. As Stonehouse (2011b, p. 10) states 'It is our role as playworkers to know and understand the rights of children, so that we can accurately advise and support children in gaining their rights.' This does not meant that the playwork practitioner needs to be an expert in law. However, they should have a general awareness of law and more importantly a working knowledge of how it directly affects their practice and the children they support.

Veracity

One concept which is not included in either ethical framework, or within the Playwork Principles (SkillsActive, 2013a), but which is equally important is the idea of veracity. Veracity is simply the concept of truth telling. As Berglund (2007) affirms, it is about being open, honest and truthful with people. Sturrock and Else (1998, p. 22) in discussing the concept of authenticity propose that playworkers need to be faithful to their feelings within play and that 'children will come to trust the "truth" of these responses'.

Veracity is also about transferring information in an accurate way, and in a way that the individual person can understand (Edwards, 2009). Article 13 of the UN Convention on the Rights of the Child (UNICEF, 1991) talks about the child's right to freedom of expression, but also the right to receive information in a media of their choosing. Playwork practitioners have a duty to listen to the children in their care and to meet their right to receive information that is truthful, honest and open through whichever media the child chooses, so that they can fully understand the information that they have requested. Do adults and even those working within playwork sometimes speak a different language, in the form of technical words or abbreviations which are not explained to children? Through doing this the playwork practitioner is excluding children from receiving information in an understandable format and failing to meet their needs and rights. All information in whatever media it is presented needs to be at the correct level and understanding for the children and families accessing that play provision.

However, as Stonehouse (2012, p. 250) states for playwork practitioners, always telling the truth may not be 'an easy principle to maintain when you are asked difficult questions or your answer may be distressing'. The playwork practitioner, therefore, has to be as truthful as they can, while balancing being sensitive to the needs of the child or young person who is asking the difficult question. It is also about the playwork practitioner being self-aware and recognising their limitations and seeking help and guidance from more experienced staff, when faced with these difficult questions. It is okay to admit to not knowing what the right answer is, as long as this is done in an open, honest and truthful way.

Conclusion

In conclusion, we have examined the important role that ethics has upon a playwork practitioner's practice, especially as the work force moves towards becoming a more professionally recognised body of practitioners. Ethical dilemmas occur constantly within everyday life and more importantly within playwork practice. Deciding upon the right course of action, and the right decision for both play and those children and young people who access playwork provision, can often feel like having to choose between the lesser of two evils. There may not be an obvious satisfactory answer which meets the expectations of all interested parties. However, the implication of not thinking in an ethical way is that decisions made may well be unsafe and unsatisfactory and could easily be detrimental to everyone involved.

Through being mindful of ethical principles and concepts when faced with dilemmas within playwork, the professional playwork practitioner will be assisted in making the best ethical decisions. Truly embracing and understanding the Playwork Principles (SkillsActive, 2013a), and applying Rowson's (2006) ethical framework as well as Beauchamp and Childress's (2013) ethical principles, will lead to better and more ethically sound decisions being made. This can only lead to more and better quality play opportunities for the children and young people that the playwork practitioner works closely with, and will assist in moving the profession forward.

Further discussion is required within the playwork community to decide whether or not either of these frameworks should be promoted and adopted, or whether a new framework designed by and for playworker practitioners needs to be developed to run alongside and complement the Playwork Principles (SkillsActive, 2013a). It is hoped that this article will prompt discussion and debate upon the subject.

Disclosure statement

No potential conflict of interest was reported by the author.

References

Aynsley-Green, A., Marshall, K., Lewsley, P., & Towler, K. (2008). *UK commissioners' report to the UN committee on the rights of the child* [Internet]. Retrieved August 26, 2015, from http://www.childcomwales.org.uk/uploads/publications/61.pdf

Banks, S., & Gallagher, A. (2009). *Ethics in professional life: Virtues for health and social care.* Basingstoke: Palgrave McMillan.

Beauchamp, T., & Childress, J. (2013). *Principles of biomedical ethics* (7th ed.). Oxford: Oxford University Press.

Berglund, C. (2007). *Ethics for health care* (3rd ed.). Oxford: Oxford University Press.

Bracknell Forest Council. (2012). *Speaking up, speaking out, taking action: A strategy for commissioning advocacy in Bracknell Forest 2012–2015* [Internet]. Retrieved August 26, 2015, from http://www.bracknell-forest.gov.uk/advocacy-commissioning-strategy.pdf

Brussoni, M., Olsen, L. L., Pike, I., & Sleet, D. A. (2012). Risky play and children's safety: Balancing priorities for optimal child development. *International Journal of Environmental Research and Public Health, 9*(9), 3134–3148.

Cole-Hamilton, I. (2008). Children's rights and play. In F. Brown & C. Taylor (Eds.), *Foundations of playwork* (pp. 234–237). Maidenhead: Open University Press.

Cottrell, S. (2008). *The study skills handbook* (3rd ed.). Basingstoke: Palgrave MacMillan.

Davy, A., & Gallagher, J. (2006). *New playwork: Play and care for children 4–16* (4th ed.). London: Delmar Cengage Learning.

Edwards, S. D. (2009). *Nursing ethics: A principle-based approach* (2nd ed.). Basingstoke: Palgrave Macmillan.

Griffith, R., & Tengnah, C. (2010). *Law and professional issues in nursing* (2nd ed.). Exeter: Learning Matters.

Hendrick, J. (2004). *Law and ethics: Foundations in nursing and health care*. Cheltenham: Nelson Thornes.

Hughes, B. (2012). *Evolutionary playwork* (2nd ed.). London: Routledge.

Hugman, R. (2005). *New approaches in ethics for the caring professions*. Basingstoke: Palgrave Macmillan.

Johns, C. (2009). *Becoming a reflective practitioner* (3rd ed.). Oxford: Blackwell.

KIDS. (2013). *Playday survey report 2013* [Internet]. Retrieved August 26, 2015, from http://www.kids.org.uk/News/kids-playday-survey-report-2013

Lundy, L. (2007). Voice is not enough: Conceptualising article 12 of the United Nations convention on the rights of the child. *British Educational Research Journal, 33*(6), 927–942.

Pithouse, A., & Crowley, A. (2007). Adults rule? Children advocacy and complaints to social services. *Children and Society, 21*, 201–213.

Plowden, L. (2010). Article 31: A playwork perspective. *Play Today.* Winter (68) p. 16.

Rowson, R. (2006). *Working ethics: How to be fair in a culturally complex world*. London: Jessica Kingsley.

SkillsActive. (2013a). Playwork principles [Internet]. Retrieved August 26, 2015, from http://www.skillsactive.com/PDF/sectors/Playwork_Principles.pdf

SkillsActive. (2013b). *SkillsActive launched Register of Playwork Professionals* [Internet]. Retrieved August 26, 2015, from http://www.skillsactive.com/news/skillsactive-launched-register-of-playwork-professionals#sthash.cDt0QjsH.dpuf

SkillsActive. (2015). *SkillsActive UK Play and Playwork Education and Skills Strategy 2011–2016* [Internet]. Retrieved August 26, 2015, from http://www.skillsactive.com/PDF/sectors/PDF_28_-Skillsactive_Playwork_Strategy_2011-2016.pdf

Stonehouse, D. (2011a). Using reflective practice to ensure high standards of care. *British Journal of Healthcare Assistants*, June. *5*(6), 299–302.

Stonehouse, D. (2011b, December 23). Advocacy and the playworker. IP-DiP: For professionals in play. *Weekly,* (80), 9–11.

Stonehouse, D. (2012). The support worker's guide to ethical practice. *British Journal of Healthcare Assistants*, May. *6*(5), 249–250.

Stonehouse, D. (2013). You are a manager: Should you be a leader? *British Journal of Healthcare Management*, August. *19*(8), 391–393.

Sturrock, G., & Else, P. (1998). The playground as therapeutic space: playwork as healing. In: *Proceedings of the IPA/USA Triennial National Conference, Play in a Changing Society: Research, Design, Application.* June 1998, Colorado, USA.

Thompson, I. E., Melia, K. M., Boyd, K. M., & Horsburgh, D. (2006). *Nursing ethics* (5th ed.). London: Churchill Livingstone Elsevier.

UNICEF. (1991). *United Nations convention on the rights of the child*. Svenska: UNICEF Kommitten.

Wragg, M. (2008). Guerilla playwork. In F. Brown & C. Taylor (Eds.), *Foundations of playwork* (pp. 169–173). Berkshire: Open University Press.

The Big Swing: reflections on the first 10 years of an adventure playground

Mike Wragg

This paper examines the life and times of the first 10 years of an adventure playground and the ways in which that playground has been affected by and responded to the opportunities and challenges presented by changes to the prevailing national and local socio-political and economic climate of that decade. The paper explores significant events in the playground's history and the ways in which those events have been influenced by the interrelationship between popular public perceptions of children and their play; the national and local policy context for children, play and playwork; and the implications of such for the playwork practice of those charged with developing and running one of the north of England's flagship playwork provisions. During the latter part of the playground's comparatively short life many of these factors have inevitably contributed to or been played out against a backdrop of ideological political and economic reform popularly termed as austerity. Although the full financial implications for small charitable organisations such as The Big Swing of the present UK government's austerity programme are only just becoming realised, the ideological neoliberal tenets by which they are informed have had a demonstrably detrimental effect on the playground's practice and delivery.

Eccleshill Adventure Playground, known locally as The Big Swing, is an open access adventure playground located in Bradford, West Yorkshire. As is typical of many former industrial towns in the north of England, Bradford suffers from comparatively high levels of socio-economic disadvantage, and is in fact the 26th most disadvantaged of the country's 354 boroughs (JSNA, 2014). During the course of its lifetime The Big Swing has consistently attracted increasing numbers of children year on year, culminating in a total of 9463 passing through its gates during the financial year 2014/2015. The Big Swing, having started life as a local authority run project, is now an independent charitable entity sitting in the heart of the local community providing a focal point for children and families. The playground pursues an approach which, whilst maintaining children's safety, does so without restricting their freedom to play in the kinds of challenging way which may be outlawed by other play provisions, to which the following testimonies bare witness:

> If there weren't all them gates here then I wouldn't be here. I wouldn't be able to come because it would just be a park like that one and there wouldn't be any playworkers to keep us safe so I wouldn't be allowed out. (eight-year-old female user)

It's nice to let them play somewhere that's not ridiculously safe. It's good that they can challenge themselves; it's what life's all about. It's BRILL! (Mother of two boys, aged eight and 10 years)

Although celebrating its 10th birthday on 8 August 2015, the project was conceived in the late winter of 2002, and as is no doubt the case with many such examples, taking a concept which existed only in the minds of a handful of enthusiastic individuals and turning it into a fully functioning, sustainable operation required a combination of good fortune, dedication, vision and money. In the first instance this vision and dedication came from a small but very committed team of Play Development Officers employed by a local authority department concerned primarily with the development of early years and childcare provision.

That department was established in 1998, under the New Labour administration, to deliver its landmark National Childcare Strategy and Sure Start Local Programme. Whilst the success of these initiatives in meeting their objectives of reducing social inequality is debateable (Lewis, 2011) they were instrumental to launching The Big Swing, as the money that came with them enabled local authorities to begin major programmes of social investment in children, young people and family services (Nursery World, 2001). However, had it not been for the foresight and commitment to children's play and playwork demonstrated by members of the department's senior management team, those with the vision to reintroduce a form of children's play provision which was regarded at the time by many as a 'thing of the past', would never have been recruited. For whilst the department's primary purpose was to develop affordable and inclusive childcare provision, the creation of open access adventure playgrounds was never an explicitly stated outcome of these government initiatives. It was very much on a local level that a forward-thinking commitment to children's play was made through the recruitment of a team of Play as well as Childcare Development Officers to deliver the National Childcare and Sure Start initiatives. The remit of these newly appointed Play Development Officers was to work with the childcare sector to improve the quality of play opportunities afforded within typical care provision and create new, open access play provision staffed by qualified playworkers. At this point it ought to be noted that those at the forefront of The Big Swing's development were all students at one time or another of the BA (Hons) Playwork course at Leeds Beckett (formerly Metropolitan) University. This relationship between The Big Swing and the University endures, with the Course Leader fulfilling the role of Chair of the playground's management committee, and the playground providing placement and volunteer opportunities as well as paid employment to many students over the last 10 years.

As mentioned earlier, this type of provision was regarded at the time as somewhat archaic. Most of the country's existing adventure playgrounds had opened during an era in which concerns for children's safety at play were less extreme than they had become in recent decades, and in which attitudes towards the risk and challenge were more permissive. However, in a modern age of strict accountability and the fear of litigation that accompanied it, along with significant funding cuts over the previous decades, those playgrounds had declined significantly in number (Chilton, 2013). Of those which remained many more had responded to this increased societal aversion to risk in children's play by gradually restricting the variety of play opportunities available to children till the point at which many of them had become safe and sanitised shadows of their former selves. So, to realise an ambitious vision that sought to re-establish play opportunities which had in the eyes of many professionals become unacceptably risky or dangerous, was not a simple task. A strong degree of commitment and integrity, combined with a sound understanding of the legislative requirements governing such provision, was vital. As was, in the face of much doubt and no little opposition, a preparedness and determination to advocate for the child's right and need to play. Nevertheless, by the late 2000s The Big Swing had become an established community provision and was described by various commentators initiated in the early adventure playground movement of the 1960s and 1970s as authentically reflective of the practice and ethos of those original examples.

This was an accolade of which the playground's early developers were justifiably proud. In remaining true to the adventure playground movement's roots the received wisdom of the time, which said that many of the play types, structures, games and activities synonymous with traditional adventure playgrounds were no longer viable in an age of health and safety obsession, had been successfully challenged. Challenging this received wisdom in the eyes of fellow professionals, funders and local policy makers involved developing a theoretic model that sought both to explode the health and safety myth and posit the argument that the consequences of its propagation were proving harmful to children's development. The playground's success and growing profile resulted in its representatives being invited, in 2008, to deliver a presentation at Play Wales' Spirit of Adventure Play Conference in Cardiff, Wales, the subject of which was this theoretic model (see Figure 1).

The model identifies the growth of this myth through a series of stages characterised by ignorance and fear which over the course of time have been so widely accepted as to become the putative norm. In the first instance the myth *emerges* in the shape of the introduction of or significant revision to legislation or policy apparently related to a particular aspect of playwork practice. In the context of this example one might identify the introduction of the Health & Safety at Work Act (1974) as a significant emergence factor; the Act, whilst not relating specifically or explicitly to adventure playgrounds was not unreasonably interpreted by those working within the profession as having implications for their practice. The myth *develops* as a lack of clarity or detailed knowledge of the legislation and its requirements lead to uncertainty and anxiety which is *reinforced* and heighted by misleading high-profile media coverage and single-issue campaigns; the principal chapter in Tim Gill's book *No fear: Growing up in a risk averse society* addresses one such example in which a popular television programme of the era supported a playground safety

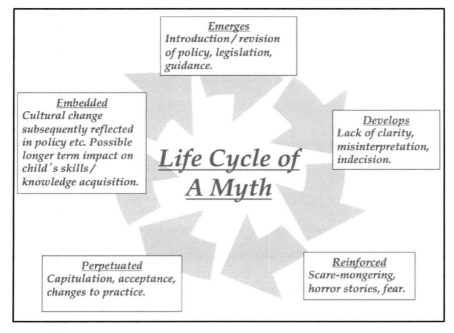

Figure 1.   Life cycle of a myth.

campaign by focussing on a particular case of an eight-year-old girl who died after falling from a swing and hitting her head on the tarmac below (Gill, 2007). Whilst this was of course a tragic accident it's important for perspective's sake to point out that on average at least one child per week dies at the hands of their parents (Jutte, 2015), whilst the number killed in playground accidents remains, despite the endeavours of the safety campaign, at approximately one per year (Layard & Dunn, 2009). Nevertheless, the myth is *perpetuated* by a general capitulation to the entrenched fear and ignorance which becomes *embedded* in the culture of playgrounds' policies, procedures and practice exemplified by modified 'safe' play equipment and the prohibition of previously acceptable play behaviours (see Figure 2).

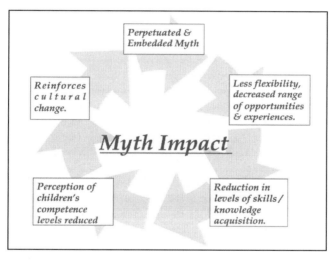

Figure 2.   Myth impact.

The implications of these modifications to the variety and range of play opportunities for children are two-fold. The first is broadly reflective of the negative cycle of compound flexibility, proposed by Brown (2003) in the publication, *Playwork theory and practice.*

It is by encountering problems and challenges in their play that children develop the range and flexibility of responses required to meet those challenges. The more varied, complex and frequently encountered the challenge, the greater the potential for the child to develop increasingly divergent, flexible and sophisticated responses. If those challenging play opportunities are removed, so too is the opportunity for children to develop the particular skills and abilities commensurate to the challenge. In a sanitised and risk-free play environment children have both fewer opportunities to develop the divergent and flexible responses required of risk-management and problem resolution, and fewer opportunities to demonstrate those skills to adults. Therefore the adult *perception* of children's capabilities is reduced and so play behaviours once typical become increasingly regarded as dangerous, and are consequently further restricted. In this negative feedback loop children become increasingly infantilised and the complexity of their play is diminished. Furthermore, as playworkers facilitate increasingly less flexible and challenging play opportunities, so too does their practice become increasingly less imaginative, unresponsive and inflexible. Much of the work of those involved with The Big Swing in its infancy was concerned with reversing this cycle which resulted in the following Risk and Play Policy Statement.

The Big Swing adventure playground recognises children's play as a biological drive and legal right as enshrined in international and domestic policy and legislation. The playground strives to give all children the opportunity, at their own discretion, to engage in the full range of play types by creating a rich and stimulating environment and by practicing a facilitative, non-directive approach.

The playground responds to the child's instinct to experience risk in their play, and whilst facilitating opportunities to do so in compliance with relevant health & safety and risk-benefit management policy and procedure, acknowledges that an element of real danger must be present for such opportunities to be truly beneficial to the child. Therefore it is inevitable that children attending the playground will incur injury.

Whilst written to be an honest assessment of the sorts of encounters playing children were likely to have at The Big Swing, the final sentence of the statement was also designed to be deliberately provocative. For during the early part of the first decade of the new millennium the popular societal construction of children and childhood was informed by a discourse of protectionism (James & James, 2004) which bore little resemblance to the prevailing attitude of comparative benign neglect which had influenced parenting and playwork practice of the previous generation's children. For example between the 1970s and 1990s the distance children were permitted to travel unaccompanied from the home had shrunk by 90%, as had the number of children travelling to school by themselves. Furthermore, the average age at which children were considered old enough to play out without adult supervision had increased from five or six years to 12 years over the same period (Gill, 2007). The perceived threat of 'stranger danger' which had previously roused levels of concern proportionate to its extremely low frequency of occurrence had, as a consequence of several high-profile and long-running stories of child abduction in the national press, reached mythical proportions. The government response was to introduce a raft of protectionist legislation such as the Protection of Children Act 1999; Criminal Records Bureau; Children Act 2004, incorporating Every Child Matters; or the Sex Offender Disclosure Scheme. These measures had a subtle yet cumulative effect of reinforcing the public perception of the child as 'at risk' thus increasing anxiety and normalising ever more restrictive parenting practices. A classic example of this media hysteria can be found in the News of the World headline which, following its long-running coverage of the abduction and murder of Sarah Payne, erroneously stated that 'EVERYONE IN BRITAIN HAS A CHILD SEX OFFENDER LIVING ONE MILE FROM THEIR HOME' (Nash & Williams, 2010). It is due to headlines such as these that 'stranger danger' has become cited by parents as one of the most significant reasons for restricting their children's freedom to play out, yet numbers of abductions of children by strangers have not increased over the course of the last generation (Savage & Charman, 2001).

In this culture of protectionism in which children became characterised by their vulnerability, stating provocatively in policy that injury was a likely natural outcome of playing proved to be a crucial element of achieving the playground originators' aims. It opened the floor to a more honest and realistic conversation about what playing should entail and focussed attention on children's capabilities and resilience rather than their supposed frailties. Consequently steering group meetings became characterised by senior officials reminiscing fondly, comparing the scars of their own adventurous childhoods and bemoaning the absence of such experiences from the lives of children today. It was also hoped that being open with parents about the playground's position might mean that they would be less likely to consider legal action should their child injure themselves. As alluded to earlier the fear of being sued had become a typical worry for children's play providers, but one which The Big Swing, in its rejection of the health and safety myth, was fairly sanguine about; not because of arrogance or complacency, but because the Health and Safety Executive itself had, in 2007, described litigation culture as a myth, and the expert guidance surrounding the relevant legislation made it clear that one need only fear litigation should they have acted negligently (HSE, 2007).

Fortuitously for The Big Swing its bid to reverse this tide of protectionism coincided with a burgeoning sea change in attitude towards children's safety emanating from some less expected but altogether more authoritative arenas. The Health and Safety Executive was exposing as myths examples of disproportionate restrictions on children's play enacted in the name of health and safety, and the cause of escalating public concerns for children's health and fitness were increasingly attributed to their sedentary risk-averse lifestyles. Writers such as Frank Furedi and Tim Gill were attracting national media attention for their warnings of the dangers of 'battery rearing' children and calls for more active, challenging and outdoor childhoods were exemplified by Paul Cornall, Head of Leisure Safety for the Royal Society for the Prevention of Accidents who advised that: ' … it is better for a child to break a wrist falling out of a tree than to get a repetitive strain wrist injury at a young age from using a computer or video games console' (Ball, Gill, & Spiegel, 2012).

By March 2006 things were looking good for The Big Swing. It was in the process of becoming a community owned charitable organisation and political support for children's play was reaching unprecedented levels as the Children's Play Initiative of the Big Lottery Fund was launched. This initiative saw the foundation of Play England, a £15 million, five-year project to support and develop children's play and a further £140 million was made available to local authorities and community groups across the country to develop local play provision. Furthermore, on 11 December 2007, the government unveiled a 10-year plan for children in England. Alongside a plethora of proposals to improve the quality of children's education, safety and general well-being, the plan contained a commitment to ensure the nation-wide development of 30 supervised adventure playgrounds, high quality training for 4000 playworkers and the creation of a national strategy for children's play. Whilst the long-term success of these initiatives, of which an in-depth analysis can be found elsewhere in this publication, is debateable, they certainly helped to raise the profile of The Big Swing which later gained prominence as a case study of good practice in the final national Children's Play Evaluation Report to the Big Lottery Fund (Voce, 2008).

During this halcyon period for play and playwork The Big Swing enjoyed a comparative abundance of public and political good will, support, resource and perhaps most importantly money. This allowed the playground to pursue unquestioningly its primary purpose of providing a stimulating play environment for children and young people and has undoubtedly provided multifarious benefits for its users. Nevertheless, the community in which it is located continues to suffer from significant social and economic deprivation. This of course isn't surprising as adventure playgrounds have historically for various reasons, including those of finance, been located in areas of multiple deprivation, and The Big Swing's environs are no different.

Bradford district is the fourth most populous metropolitan district in England, has the third highest number of 0–15 year-olds (123,800) in the country, and is one of the most deprived boroughs in the UK (ranking 26th of 354 nationally) (JSNA, 2014). Bradford has the youngest population outside London (nearly 25% of the population) and the rate of child poverty as well as the increase in child population in acutely deprived areas is set to increase rapidly (JSNA, 2014). Rates of teenage conceptions are twice as high in the most deprived quintile of the population (49.2 per 1000 population compared to 22.1 for the least deprived). Children born to teenage parents are more likely to experience poverty and poor health outcomes that, without intervention, have created a negative cycle whereby each generation suffers increasingly poor health outcomes (JSNA, 2014). Higher proportions of disabled children, and children with special educational needs (SEN) live in poverty and their numbers are concentrated in areas of high deprivation. The costs associated with caring for a disabled child, and the difficulties parents face in obtaining and maintaining work, make it difficult for these families to move out of poverty (JSNA, 2014). Fifty-nine thousand and nine hundred adults across the Bradford district have no qualifications. This equates to around 18% of the working age population, which is higher than both the regional and national average. Rates of unemployment among the adult population are high and residents from black and minority ethnic (BME) communities are disproportionately affected (JSNA, 2014).

Against this bleak backdrop of social inequality, by the late 2000s the outlook for The Big Swing was beginning to look less than encouraging. Those early revenue streams, and the hope and optimism for the future of play and playwork that accompanied them, were beginning to dry up, and by 2010 a new Tory-led coalition government was embarking on an austerity programme of savage cuts to local authority budgets and public funding for children's play. Indeed, the previous Labour government's Playbuilder programme was frozen by the newly elected Education Secretary, Michael Gove, within months of taking up the position in 2010, and the subsequent year's allocation of the now deceased fund were reduced by 28%. Local authority capital budgets for children's play facilities have fallen by an average of 69%, equating to approximately £330,000 over the three years between 2010 and 2013, and Bradford Metropolitan District Council, home of The Big Swing, has received the country's largest cut of £1.2 million, over three times the national average. Revenue budgets have also fallen across the country by an average of 60% and the Director of Play England predicts that the consequences of these swingeing cuts will be the total annihilation of adventure playgrounds in England within the next three years (Jozwiak, 2014). The Big Swing's response has been to diversify its provision in order to appeal to a wider variety of potential income streams, and to sell private group bookings, usually to schools. So far this strategy has proved to be relatively successful with a number of small contracts having been won to tackle issues of unemployment and school exclusion in the local community. However, the viability of the playground's longer-term future based on this type of piecemeal, hand-to-mouth existence is anything but certain. Furthermore, I discussed in a chapter entitled Guerrilla Playwork, in the publication *Foundations of Playwork*, examples of adventure playgrounds which have succumbed to this funding model's potential to compromise their original objectives and child-centred ethos (Wragg, 2008). Equally if not more concerning, however, is the forced privatisation of play sessions at the expense of those children for whom the playground was originally established. This upward redistribution of goods and services towards those who can afford to pay and away from those who cannot is reflective of the inevitable and, many would argue, not unintended consequence of the government's wider austerity programme.

The austerity agenda in this context is regarded as an essential plank of neoliberal reform. This refers to a theory of political and economic practices, which propose that the common good is best served by reducing public spending, promoting private ownership and maximising the reach and frequency of competitive market transactions. The rise of contemporary neoliberalism as the dominant force in British politics can be attributed to the policies initiated during the Premiership of Margaret Thatcher (1979–1990), and strengthened throughout the 1980s by her unofficial transatlantic partnership with President Reagan. Whilst initially concerned primarily with matters of commerce and industry, such as market deregulation and the weakening of trade union powers, policies of the neoliberal revolution, as it has been described, sought also to drive principles of competition into the heart of public policy (Harvey, 2005).

The Conservative-led coalition government sought to advance the revolution with alacrity by justifying further public spending cuts as a necessary cure for the nation's economic ills, and introducing legislation such as the Education Act (2011) and Health and Social Care Act (2012), which pave the way for greater private ownership of public services. Whether one chooses to believe the government's deficit reduction rhetoric or not, an undeniable outcome of these neoliberal policies is to further disadvantage the already marginalised, vulnerable and poor; particularly the nation's poorest children. As this paper is written the Supreme Court has ruled that the UK government's reforms to welfare expenditure breach the United Nations Convention on the Rights of the Child (Butler, 2015), and forecasts predict that child poverty in the UK will increase by a third in the decade to 2020, to its highest level in a generation (Doward & Helm, 2015).

So, the country's poorest children are set to become poorer, increasing the need for services such as The Big Swing which are already struggling on reduced budgets. Yet the costs to the playground of the government's fervent pursuit of neoliberal reform are felt more widely than simple reductions to income. The inherent consequences of excessive individualism and competitiveness associated with neoliberalism has led to partnerships between local authority departments and third-sector organisations such as The Big Swing breaking down as they seek to out-compete one another for the meagre resources available to them. For a community in which numbers of families are more reliant than the national average on welfare, The Big Swing seems to be experiencing the fall-out of reduced household incomes. In the last 12 months the playground has been broken into three times losing thousands of pounds worth of equipment leading to a potentially unaffordable increase in insurance premiums. Furthermore, The Big Swing is now facing its first litigious claim which comes from a parent with whom the playground has enjoyed a good relationship for the last eight years, and whose 12-year-old son has been a regular attendee since he was five years old. One may surmise that in the present era of austerity the appeal of receiving a few thousand pounds in compensation outweighs the likely potential loss of this community facility. Inevitably the thought of a family that has effectively benefitted from free childcare, amongst all the other opportunities The Big Swing has provided, bringing the playground to its knees, sticks in the collective craw of all those who have worked together for the last 12 years to deliver this project. However, what is even more galling is that the playground's strict adherence to the best practice principles of risk-benefit assessment as endorsed in the guidance of national authorities on the subject such as the Play Safety Forum, Play England and the Health and Safety Executive apparently counts for nothing in the eyes of the insurance companies. Even if The Big Swing manages to survive the impact of budget cuts and increased insurance premiums the quality of play opportunities available to children will undoubtedly suffer. Already the playground's insurers are demanding that 'dangerous' play structures upon which thousands of children have played for over a decade without issue, are modified or demolished. If The Big Swing is to survive it will almost certainly do so on a reduced allocation of staff, all of whom will have suffered the cost of helping to provide for the child's right to play.

Disclosure statement

No potential conflict of interest was reported by the author.

References

Ball, D., Gill, T., & Spiegel, B. (2012). *Managing risk in play provision: Implementation guide*. London: Play England.
Brown, F. (2003). Compound flexibility: The role of playwork in child development. In F. Brown (Ed.), *Playwork theory and practice* (pp. 51–65). Buckingham: Open University Press.

Butler, P. (2015, March 18). UK benefits cap is lawful but breaches UN children's rights obligations. *The Guardian*, p. 22.

Chilton, T. (2013). *Adventure playgrounds: A brief history.* Retrieved August 2015, from http://www. fairplayforchildren.org/pdf/1397922953.pdf

Doward, J., & Helm, T. (2015, June 20). Child poverty rise across Britain halts 'Progress made since 1990s' *The Guardian*, p. 17.

Gill, T. (2007). *No fear: Growing up in a risk averse society.* London: Calouste-Gulbenkian Foundation.

Harvey, D. (2005). *A brief history of Neoliberalism.* Oxford: Oxford University Press.

HSE. (2007). *HSC welcomes demolition of compensation culture myth.* Retrieved August 2014, from http://www.hse.gov.uk/press/2004/c04023.htm

James, A., & James, A. (2004). *Constructing childhood. Theory, policy & social practice.* Basingstoke: Palgrave McMillan.

Jozwiak, G. (2014, January 7–20). Outdoor play under threat from funding cull. *Children and Young People Now.*

JSNA. (2014). *Bradford & airdale joint strategic needs assessment.* Bradford: Bradford Metropolitan District Council.

Jutte, S. et al. (2015). *How safe are our children? The most comprehensive overview of child protection in the UK.* London: NSPCC.

Layard, R., & Dunn, J. (2009). *A good childhood: Searching for values in a competitive age.* London: Penguin Books Ltd.

Lewis, J. (2011). From sure start to children's centres: An analysis of policy change in English early years programmes. *Journal of Social Policy, 40,* 71–88.

Nash, M., & Williams, A. (2010). *Handbook of public protection.* Abingdon: Willan Publishing.

Nursery World. (2001). A parent's guide to the national childcare strategy. Retrieved August 2015, from http://www.nurseryworld.co.uk/nursery-world/news/1085658/parents-guide-national-childcare-strategy

Savage, S., & Charman, S. (2001). Public protectionism and 'Sarah's law'. Exerting pressure through single issue campaigns. In M. Nash & A. Williams (Eds.), *Handbook of public protection* (pp. 434–455). Abingdon: Taylor and Francis.

Voce, A. (2008). The state of play in England. In F. Brown & C. Taylor (Eds.), *Foundations of playwork* (pp. 22–26). Maidenhead: McGraw-Hill.

Wragg, M. (2008). Guerrilla playwork. In F. Brown & C. Taylor (Eds.), *Foundations of playwork* (pp. 169–174). Maidenhead: McGraw-Hill.

Books worth (re)reading

Adventure playgrounds, by Jack Lambert and Jenny Pearson, Harmondsworth, Penguin Books, 1974, 176pp.

The first substantial book reflecting on the subject of adventure playgrounds was a 'personal account of a play-leader's work' by Jack Lambert, as told to Jenny Pearson. The book, *Adventure Playgrounds* appeared in 1974, and recounted Lambert's experiences of developing projects all over England, with the aid of a three-year grant from the Joseph Rowntree Memorial Trust. Because it was published by a mainstream publisher (Penguin Books), it naturally drew a wider audience than many of the more academic texts that have followed. However, that is not to suggest the book lacks substance, or ignores any theoretical underpinning to the work. Indeed early on in the book they tell us:

> The adventure playground is free space, space where children can do things they are normally prevented from doing. There is a whole world of difference between this and the 'familiar, dull, unimaginatively equipped, asphalted flat squares or triangles' (Holme & Massie, 1970) provided by most local authorities. As T.H. Sorensen, the Danish architect whose idea it first was, described the dream in 1931, 'A junk playground in which child could create and shape, dream and imagine a reality.'

We long ago stopped referring to such people as 'play-leaders', because the core philosophy of the work is essentially 'hands-off'. Playworkers, as they are now called, focus on the child's agenda, rather than any specific set of adult priorities. That is one of the things that makes playwork unique. Lambert was one of the first people to articulate that view fully. His approach was basically to provide a space, fill it with odds and ends, building materials, pots and pans and a watchful (but not intrusive) adult. Then he just let the children get on with it. He suggests the success of the role 'hangs on being able to give without expecting any return for it'. That philosophy is evident throughout the book, which contains one powerful quote after another from the children themselves. For example:

> Edgar, from Parkhill: There was me, my mate Jim, Sam, Willy and my little brother. We drew some plans but we didn't go by them really. This was what I was thinking about, that was what the others were thinking of, so we put them together and just built it as we went along. We sort of thought 'that'd look good there' so we done it. We incorporated wooden beams in the four corners and built up the sides on top of the brick wall with wood – old floor boards mostly.
>
> Maxine, from West Ham: It's very good over here, though, because you can go on all the things, do what you like. Indoors, in your house, you haven't got anything to do – well, you have to come over here to play, don't you? My house is only a little one. I've got four brothers and my brother Alan, he's the oldest, he comes here a lot. Sometimes I'm here at 9 o'clock and then I get home and my Mum tells me off, but she don't tell me off very much.

Lambert's philosophy of working with the child's agenda is also demonstrated through his own reflections. For example:

As summer drew close, there was talk of an Open Day. The committee wanted to organize a barbecue. However, I said, 'Let's have an Open Day by all means. But why not introduce the idea to the children and get them to do it? Let *them* have the ideas as well.' The kids came up with some fantastic ideas and I just said, 'Great! Go ahead and do it!' They wanted music, so I cadged some cable and ran a power line over to the site from a near-by house for a record player.

The authors recount the success of Lambert's methods in a range of very different communities around the country. In so doing, they demonstrate how the freedom experienced by children on these adventure playgrounds enables them to develop initiative, creativity and a new understanding of their immediate environment. All this is confirmed by the children's own reflections.

Lambert introduces us to powerful lessons about adventure playgrounds, some of which were learnt from 'a disappointment' in Welwyn. He suggests that adventure playgrounds should be open until late in the evening, and that the workers should make every effort to become part of the local community that they are serving. He says they are most suited to communities where children are short of space; where they do not have gardens and where the playground can be sited close to housing, so that small children do not have to walk long distances in the dark during the winter. He also highlights the additional need for good quality provision for older teenagers, otherwise they will come to dominate the adventure playground, with the result that smaller children will stay away.

This book takes us back to a very different age, to a time before the Health & Safety at Work Act (1974); to a world with no games consoles and no Internet and with far fewer distractions to occupy children's time. Nevertheless, the book has real relevance today. In a world where we have become over-protective of children, but at the same time fearful of them, the need for a safe space where they are able to be themselves, is greater now than ever before. We know that children today are more inactive, and often more isolated, than their predecessors, and so there is still a widespread need for the 'fun, freedom and flexibility' that an adventure playground offers (Brown, 2014). Lambert and Pearson offer us insights into a world where children have real ownership of their play, in a 'home from home' environment that offers adventure in every sense of the word.

References

Brown, F. (2014). *Play and playwork: 101 stories of children playing*. Maidenhead: Open University Press.
The Health and Safety at Work Act Etc. (1974). London: HMSO.
Holme, A., & Massie, P. (1970). *Children's play: A study of needs and opportunities*. London: Michael Joseph.

Fraser Brown

Index

Note: **Boldface** page numbers refer to tables &
italic page numbers refer to figures. Page
numbers followed by "n" refer to endnotes.

Activity Sheffield 32, 33, 35
adulteration 88
adventure playgrounds 34–7, 75, 119–20; in
    England 116; open access playwork 93, 111;
    traditional 93, 112
Adventure Playgrounds (Lambert & Pearson)
    119–20
'age of austerity' 72
anti-poverty strategy 75, 79
'Argument for Playwork, The' 5
austerity, in UK 38–9, 78–82; as opportunity 19;
    playwork in times 15–19; politics of 18;
    programme 14; as threat 18

Balls, Ed 24
Battram, Arthur 19, 72, 78, 80–2
Beauchamp, T. 104–6
Beck, Ulrich 72
beneficence, ethical principles 105–6
'Best Play' objectives 27, **28**
Big Lottery Fund (BLF): Children's Play
    Initiative 115; play projects 33, 78; programme
    evaluation 18; *see also Children's Play
    Programme*
Big Swing: austerity agenda 116; Bradford
    district 110, 115–16; Children's Play Initiative
    of Big Lottery Fund 115; children's safety
    110–11; community provision 111, 115;
    culture of protectionism 114–15; development
    111; impact of budget cuts 116–17; "life cycle
    of a myth" 112, *112*; "myth impact" 113, *113*;
    play opportunities and challenges 111, 113;
    revenue budgets 116; Risk and Play Policy
    Statement 113–14; social investment 111;
    'stranger danger' 114
binary thinking in playwork 73–4
Blair, Tony 24, 74
BLF *see* Big Lottery Fund
Bracknell Forest Council 106
Bradford district 110, 115–16

Bristol City Council 53
Brown, Fraser 4, 5, 89, 91, 95
Brown, Gordon 24

Cameron, David 24
Cardiff, children's street presence in 56, **57**
Childcare Development Officers 111
Child Poverty Strategy for Scotland 79
children: agenda, Lambert's philosophy of
    119–20; geographies of 14, 15; imagination
    as 11–13
Children's Play Council (CPC) 4, 6, 8n6, 22,
    24, 25n5
Children's Play Information Service (CPIS) 16
Children's Play Policy Forum (CPPF) 5, 39
Children's Play Programme: 'Best Play'
    objectives 27, 28, **28**; Big Lottery Fund
    27–30; Department for Children, Schools
    and Families 28–9; early intervention
    programmes 29; in England 30; local-level
    evaluation 29; national evaluation of 29; Sure
    Start Programme 29
Children's Rights Alliance for England (CRAE) 4
Childress, J. 104–6
child well-being, UNICEF study 79
Clegg, Nick 25
Cloodle 64
Community and Youth Workers Union (CYWU) 5
complex adaptive system 72, 73
Conservative Party 24
Conway, Mick 15
Cornall, Paul 115
CPC *see* Children's Play Council
CPPF *see* Children's Play Policy Forum
CRAE *see* Children's Rights Alliance for
    England
CYWU *see* Community and Youth Workers
    Union

Davy, A. 87, 88, 106
Department for Children, Schools and Families
    (DCSF) 28–9, 80; National Play Strategy 80
do-it-yourself (DIY) approach 62, *62*
Don Valley Athletics Stadium 36

Early Intervention Grant (EIG) 33
Eccleshill Adventure Playground *see*
Big Swing
Education Act (2011) 116
EIG *see* Early Intervention Grant
Elliot, Anthony 72
Else, Perry 5, 6, 7n2
England: adventure playgrounds in 116;
children's play provision in 29, 30;
Government and National Lottery
spending 22, **23**; National Play Strategy
for 22
English National Play Strategy 77
Erikson, E. H. 86
ethical principles: Beauchamp, T. 104–6;
beneficence 105–6; Childress, J. 104–6;
F.A.I.R 103–4; justice 106; non-maleficence
106; respect for autonomy 104–5
ethics, definition of 101

F.A.I.R., Rowson's ethical framework 103–4
Ferguson, Alice 19, 52, 54
Firestein, S. 65
Fisher, Katherine 87, 88, 90, 94
Foundations of Playwork (Brown & Taylor)
3, 4, 116
free play opportunities 56; legislation 58–9;
locational criteria 57; play distances 57–8;
play strategies 58; street playgrounds
58–9, *59*
'fun, freedom and flexibility' 120
Furedi, Frank 115

Geographic Information System 57
Geographies of Children, Youth and Families
Research Group 15
Gertz, E. 69
Getting Serious About Play (GSAP) 27, 28
Gill, Tim 16, 18, 77–81, 112, 115
Gleason, Tracy R. 10; imaginative play 11–12;
memories of play 10–11
global financial crisis 24
Go Play programme 79
Go 2 Play programme 79
Gove, Michael 116
Government and National Lottery 22, **23**
'government and play', SW England *vs.* Scotland
43, 44
GSAP *see* Getting Serious About Play
Guardian newspaper 24

Hart, Roger 7
Health and Safety Executive 114, 115, 117
Health and Social Care Act (2012) 116
Health & Safety at Work Act (1974) 112, 120
Henricks, T. 86, 87
Highfields Adventure Playground 36, 78
Holloway, S. 82

Holmes, Oliver Wendell 73
Homeless Play Project 33
Hughes, Bob 5, 6, 88, 92–3, 95
Hurst, D. K. 73

identity formation 85, 86
imagination companion, in children:
development 11–13; harnessing 12; social
interactions and 12
Inspiring Scotland 79
International Journal of Play 16
'investment years', legacy of 78–9

Jacobs, Jane 53, 73
Joswiak, G. 45
Jowell, Tessa 27
justice, ethical principles 106
Justo, P. D. 69
Juxtallage 64, 65

King, Malcolm 75

Labour Government 24
Labour Party 23, 25n5
Lambert, Jack 119–20
legislation, play environment 58–9
Lehman Bros, bankruptcy of 24
Leichter-Saxby, Morgan 93
libertarianism 92
local authorities 28
London Borough of Islington 23
Long, Alexandra 18, 78, 79, 81
Lyons, Kelda 94

Martin, Chris 18, 80, 81
McKendrick, John 18, 80, 81
Meares, Clair 91–3, 96
Moss, Peter 72

National Childcare Strategy 4, 111
National Children's Bureau (NCB) 5, 6
National City of Sport, The 36
National Lottery spending programme 22–4,
23, 27, 40
national play agencies 23
National Playing Fields Association 5
National Play Strategy for England 22
national programme design 29
NCB *see* National Children's Bureau
negative capability 87–8, 90, 96, 97
neo-liberal capitalism 72
New Labour Government's Every Child Matters
policy 4
No fear: Growing up in a risk averse society
(Gill) 112
non-maleficence, ethical principles 106

Open Method of Coordination 40, 81

Page, Angie 19, 52
'parents and play', SW England *vs.* Scotland 44–5
Payne, Sarah 114
Pearson, Jenny 119–20
personal creativity 94–5
Pitsmoor Adventure Playground 35, 36, 79
Playbuilder programme 15, 33, 116
Playday 24, 39
Play Development Officers 111
Play England 5, 6, 8n3, 8n6, 17, 24, 25, 115–17
playfulness 61; 'civic science' 63; curiosity 61;
    do-it-yourself approach 62, *62*; 'explorer of the
    world' playshop 63–4, *65–7*; 'exploring borders
    through art' playshop 64–5, *68*; flying kites and
    balloons, play role 67, *69*; 'for the love of mess'
    65–7; Touch|Play|Learn 63, *64*; wonderment 61
Playing Out (Ferguson) 52–4
'play intelligence' 79–80
Play in Times of Austerity seminar 32
'play-leaders' 119
'Play Pathfinder' programme 4
Play Safety Forum 117
Play Scotland 16, 79
Play Strategy (2008) 4, 6, 58, 80
Play Sufficiency Duty 18
playwork 3–4; as emerging profession 5; local
    authority funding 4; national body for 5;
    principles 6–7; voice 7
Playworkers Association, The 5
playwork identities: adulteration 88;
    anarchic expressions 87; awareness 94–5;
    communications 87; conversations 88;
    experiences of 93–4; fields-of-relationships *86*;
    home to playwork 91–3; identity formation
    85, 86; methodology 89–90; negative
    capability 87–8, 90, 96, 97; personal creativity
    94–5; relationships with playground 95–6; self
    communications 90–1; self-questioning 96;
    self-revealing 90, 96; uncertainty
    experience 96; vocational activity 86
Playwork in Times of Austerity seminar 15–16
Playwork People survey populations 40, 41, **42**
playwork practitioner: advocates for 106–7;
    aims of 104; decision-making process 102;
    environment impact 101; ethics of 101–3;
    importance of 105; promote children's
    rights 101; 'respect people's autonomy 103;
    role of 103; SkillsActive strategy 102;
    two-way impact 105; veracity for 107–8; *see
    also* ethical principles
playwork principles 6–7, 16 *see also* ethical
    principles
Playwork theory and practice
    (Brown) 113
Playwork Voices (Russell) 88
Plowden, L. 103
Public Laboratory for Open Technology and
    Science (Public Lab) 63–4, *66, 67*

Regalado, Cindy 19, 81, 82
Register of Playwork Professionals 5
respect for autonomy, ethical principles 104–5
Revenue Support Grant (RSG) 33
Rights of Child (Article 23) 103
Risk and Play Policy Statement 113–14
Rix, Simon 92, 94, 95
Road Traffic Regulation Act (1984) 58
Rowson, R. 103–4, 106, 108
Royal Geographical Society 15
RSG *see* Revenue Support Grant
Russell, Wendy 92–4, 96

Science has no Borders (ScHNB) 63; 'explorer
    of the world' playshops 63–4, *65–7*; 'exploring
    borders through art' playshops 64–5, *68*; 'for
    the love of mess' 65–7; Touch|Play|Learn
    63, *64*
Scotland: National Play Strategy 18; *see also*
    SW England *vs.* Scotland
Sculptorade 64
Seath, Joel 95–6
self communication 90–1
self-completion survey, in *Playwork People* 40, 41
Sensosketch 64
Sheffield, support for children's play: Activity
    Sheffield 32, 33; adventure playgrounds
    34–6; BIG Lottery for projects 33; children's
    activities (2008–13) 33; City Council 35;
    financial expenditure in 32; Highfields
    Adventure Playground 36; long-established
    charity, death of 34; Pitsmoor Adventure
    Playground 35, 36; Play Partnership in 33;
    play-related activities 33; Sharrow Community
    Forum 36; strategic-level support 33;
    summit 6; Sure Start programme 33–4;
    Woolley, Helen 77, 80, 81
simmering tensions 78
SkillsActive strategy 5, 6, 102
Smith, Chris 23, 79
Special Needs Project 34
SPICE model 89
'stranger danger' 114
strategic playwork 81; age of austerity
    72; binary thinking 73–4; bounded
    predictability 72; childhood safety 72;
    children 72–5; complex system 72, 73;
    critical pragmatism 74; environmental
    playwork 74; intervention playwork 73–4;
    lost world 71–2; neo-liberal capitalism 72;
    precarity 73; social programme 72; systemic
    playwork 74–5
street play 52; annual street party 53; movement
    in UK 39; playgrounds 58–9, *59*; *Playing Out*
    model 52–4; promoting 54–5; volunteer-driven
    model of 52
sub-national play organisations 39
Sure Start local programmes 29, 33–4, 111

SW England *vs.* Scotland: communities and play 45; dissatisfaction levels 43; 'government and play' 43, 44; opinion in 45; 'parents and play' 44–5; playspace 45; Play Strategy 49; playwork practitioners in *44, 45, 47,* 47–8; satisfaction with play (2013) *43,* 46, *46;* service provided by 46, *46;* survey population 41, 42, **42**; workplace 45–8
systemic playwork 74–5

Taylor, C. 4
Temporary Play Street Order 53–4
Thatcher, Margaret 58, 116
Tools for Conviviality (Illich) 73
Tools for Thought (Waddington) 73

UN Convention on the Rights of the Child (CRC) 6; article 31 of 5
UNICEF study 24, 79
United Kingdom (UK) 27, 29; children's play in 14, 39; decision-making, playspace provision and 80–1; evidence-based policy in 79; Gill, Tim 77–9; 'global' experience of play 48; intelligence play 79–80; 'investment years', legacy of 78–9; National Lottery in 40; national narrative for play 16–17; national play associations 17; national play intelligence in 39–40; play in contemporary 77–8; play landscape 15; play sector 16–17; Playwork in Times of Austerity seminar 15–16; playwork practitioners 39, 77; public provision of playspace 17; research design 40–2; rethinking play and society 19; society service, play in 79; 'staying the same' 48; street play movement in 39; temporal focus 41; *see also* austerity, in UK
'Unite the Union' 5

Valentine, G. 82
vocational activity 86

Ward, Colin 82
Weber, M. 86
Wheway, Rob 19, 78, 80
Willetts, David 24
Woolley, Helen 18, 77, 79–81

young people: authoritative annual survey (2008–9) 23; autonomy of 105; and local community 29; physical activity in 52